A PRACTICAL APPLICATION OF DARK PSYCHOLOGY

IDENTIFY GASLIGHTING, ANALYZE BODY LANGUAGE, AND UNCOVER MIND CONTROL TECHNIQUES TO DEFEND YOURSELF AGAINST A NARCISSIST

COLE PEARCE

This is dedicated to all who have been stepped on by those they trusted.

It is time for you to heal, forgive, and move forward.

CONTENTS

Introduction   ix

1. WHAT IS DARK PSYCHOLOGY AND WHY YOU NEED IT   1
   What is Dark Psychology?   2
   Who Uses Dark Psychology and Manipulation   2
   The Areas That Dark Psychology Is Used In   3
   Using Dark Psychology for Social Manipulation   3
   Using Dark Psychology in Dating   4
   Using Dark Psychology in Seduction   4
   Using Dark Psychology in Groups   5
   Using Dark Psychology in Business   6
   Using Dark Psychology in Politics   6
   Using Dark Psychology in War   7
   What benefits can you expect, if you understand and
   apply dark psychology   8
   Common Myths About Dark Psychology   10
   In Summary   12

2. THE ART OF PERSUASION – HOW TO GET WHAT
   YOU WANT   13
   What is persuasion, and how does it work?   13
   What Are Some Examples Of Persuasion?   14
   The Six Principles of Persuasion   15
   What Skills Do You Need To Make You More Persuasive?   18
   How To Improve Persuasion Skills?   18
   Traits and behaviors of highly persuasive people   20
   In Summary   26

3. NARCISSISM AND THE DARK TRIAD   27
   What is Narcissism?   28
   How many types of narcissism are there?   29
   What is the Dark Triad?   33
   The Dark Triad Study   35
   How to tell if someone has dark triad traits   37
   What is the Light Triad?   38
   In Summary   39

4. IDENTIFYING AND DEALING WITH A NARCISSIST   42
   Why is life with a narcissist so hard?   42
   How to know if someone is a narcissist   46
   Dealing with a narcissist   50
   Leaving a narcissist   54
   Why leaving a narcissist is so hard   54
   How to leave a narcissist   56
   Allow Yourself Time To Heal   58
   In Summary   58

5. GASLIGHTING: A NARCISSIST'S STRONGEST TOOL   60
   Gaslighting: What it is and what it's not   61
   Gaslighting vs. Manipulation   62
   Gaslighting vs. Narcissism (or Simply Being a Jerk)   62
   Gaslighting vs. a Healthy Romantic Attachment   63
   Gaslighting vs. Occasional Bad Behavior   63
   Typical scenarios where a narcissist would use
   gaslighting   64
   Why is gaslighting so dangerous for victims?   68
   Signs of Gaslighting   69
   What to do when you think somebody is gaslighting
   you   71
   In Summary   76

6. HOW TO IDENTIFY AND PROTECT YOURSELF FROM
   CHRONIC LIARS   77
   Reasons for Telling Lies   77
   Verbal Hints of a Liar   79
   Non-verbal Hints of a Liar   81
   Pathological Liars   83
   How to Deal with a Narcissistic Liar   85
   In summary   88

7. MANAGING BODY LANGUAGE AND UNDERSTANDING
   MIRRORING   89
   Body Language Basics   89
   What Is Body Language?   90
   How to Read Body Language   91
   Facial Expressions   93
   How to Read Facial Expressions   93
   Universal Expressions   93
   Micro-Expressions   94
   Identify Facial Expressions by Facial Feature   95

Using Body Language to Increase Your Confidence   96
The Body Language of a Narcissist   99
Why Narcissists Love to Mirror You   102
In Summary   104

8. FLIP IT AROUND: HOW NARCISSISTS USE MIND
CONTROL TO MANIPULATE YOU AND HOW YOU CAN
DEFEND YOURSELF   105
How does narcissistic mind control work? (Lancer,
2020)   106
Dominance vs. Balance in Relationships   106
How Your Partner Controls Your Brain   107
The mind control techniques narcissists use on you   107
How to defend yourself against narcissistic mind
control and regain your freedom   110
In Summary   112

A Message to You, the Reader!   113
Afterword   115
References   121

INTRODUCTION

Do you feel like a pawn in someone else's chess game? Are you constantly wondering whether your decisions are your own? Do you feel trapped in your relationship and can't find a way out? If so, there's a good chance that you're a victim of dark psychology.

The word "dark" and "psychology" used together to describe one concept might be difficult to wrap your head around. Most people like to believe that they are good people, which means that there is no darkness in their minds. But the reality is every human has a dark side – some people just use this darkness more than others. There is nothing wrong with having dark thoughts, and having a dark side does not mean you are a bad person. The problem comes when a person utilizes their dark side for their own malicious benefits, despite the negative implications it may have on others. The dark side turns into something dangerous when a person uses it to their advantage to manipulate and control others.

One of the biggest reasons we struggle with dark psychology is that we don't fully understand it. Dark psychology runs deeper than someone's thoughts or behaviors. It's about delving into why some people are *darker* than others. Just like psychology, it aims to find a reason as to why some people act and think the way they do. The only difference is that dark psychology focuses on why a person would intentionally harm others. For example, dark psychology examines why Adolf Hitler carried out a holocaust and killed millions of people. It asks questions like how did his brain function? And why did he target the Jews? Dark psychology can also help you understand the behavior of someone in your life. For example, if you feel like you are being manipulated by your partner, you can learn about the techniques they're using and the reason for their behavior. Dark psychology will not only help you understand the person but also how to protect yourself from them.

I wrote this book to demystify dark psychology and equip you with the knowledge to protect yourself against it. As a victim of dark psychology, I understand the helplessness that accompanies abuse. Dark psychology is common in our everyday lives and affects people from all walks of life in various ways. We see dark psychology at work with people in dysfunctional relationships with partners that manipulate them in obvious ways. But they remain in those toxic relationships because they seem to be under some sort of spell. We see dark psychology used amongst kids who make friends with other children that influence them in terrible ways despite their solid upbringing. They repeatedly make the same wrong choices, and their parents are left baffled by the control these supposed friends have over their child.

My experience as a victim of dark psychology began with a stranger that became my narcissistic best friend. We met at a training course, and I was instantly drawn to his charisma. Looking back on this time in my life, I can see all the red flags. He complimented me far too much (the friendship equivalent to love-bombing) and controlled my every move. He was incredibly jealous and completely changed as a person when I began dating (my current wife). He was unnecessarily nasty to our friends and had no time for my problems when I was having a bad day. He played my insecurities against me, blamed me for his wrongdoings, and distorted my words until I didn't even know the truth anymore. When my relationship with my partner got serious, he tried to jeopardize it by spinning stories and manipulating the truth to cause a rift between her and me. I would constantly make excuses for him because he played the victim card with me and guilted me into always taking his side. Many people wondered why I stayed friends with him when he treated me terribly. In so many ways, we were a great match. We enjoyed the same things and had a lot in common (it turns out this is because he was mirroring everything about me). He had a sob story of a childhood (a completely fabricated tale) that made me feel like I needed to protect him, a project for me, a soul to save. I know now that I was so blinded by his influence that I was actually the project for him, a soul to suck dry.

I eventually got married and, to my wife's dismay, continued my friendship with him. However, it was the beginning of the end. When I went on my honeymoon, he called me continually with apparent emergencies. He couldn't even let me have a week to celebrate my marriage without making everything about him. He was always tangled up in his own self-loathing and in constant crisis mode. This was merely a ploy to get me away from my family and to spend time with him. If there was no drama in his life, he created it and made sure he was always at the center. The day the "friendship" ended was when I finally stood up to him. He had meddled in my marriage for the last time, and I reached a point where I could no longer deal with his conceited ways. Thinking we were both adults, I calmly told him that I was happy to remain friends, but some boundaries needed to be implemented. I told him that I would no longer be his doormat, be blamed for all his actions, or be at his every beck and call. Well, that was the end of our friendship. It ended in a dramatic, action-movie-explosion kind of way. I challenged him, and he exploded. Needless to say, we are no longer friends, and I am more than well off for it. It took years of abuse to finally reach a point where I couldn't take it anymore.

I'm telling you this story because I've been there, and I've made it out to the other side. I know how scary it feels to stand up to someone using dark psychology, which is why I wrote this book. My aim is to help you regain your independence and freedom. I want you to know that you may feel like you're in a dark place now, but there is light at the end of the tunnel.

Here is a look at some of the topics we will cover throughout this book.

1. Dark Psychology: What It Is and Why You Need It

Before diving into the different sections of dark psychology and the manipulation tactics that narcissists use, it is important to understand what dark psychology truly is and how to use it to your advantage.

2. The art of persuasion: How to Get What You Want

Being persuasive is not necessarily bad. Learning the traits of persuasive people and the skills needed to persuade will help you effectively convince others to get what you want.

3. Narcissism and the Dark Triad

Three primary personalities make up the dark triad, with narcissism being the most common. Narcissism can appear in many different forms and variations. It is important to understand the narcissistic spectrum to identify what kind of narcissist you may be dealing with.

4. Identifying and Dealing with a Narcissist

A narcissist will do anything to keep their disguise. But once you know what red flags to look out for, you can unmask them and deal with them accordingly.

5. Gaslighting: A Narcissist's Strongest Tool

Gaslighting is a mind control technique that is as dangerous as it is hard to expose because the lines between gaslighting, manipulation, and simply being a jerk are often blurry.

6. How to Identify and Protect Yourself from Chronic Liars

Lying is a common tool used by dark psychologists, and there are many signs you can look out for when attempting to identify a liar.

7. Managing Body Language and Understanding Mirroring

An individual's body language and facial expression can tell a lot about their thoughts and feelings. This knowledge also gives enormous power to those who know how to use their posture, expressions, and movements to create a curated version of themselves.

8. How Narcissists Use Mind Control to Manipulate You and How You Can Defend Yourself

Some may laugh mind control off as a ridiculous idea from a 1960s spy movie. However, mind control does work. Some people need to study psychological concepts to understand how to apply it. But for narcissists and individuals with dark triad traits, it often comes naturally. Thankfully, there are ways to defend yourself against it.

The methods described in this book have helped me deal with a narcissist and heal from the trauma. I have spent years piecing together my experience and knowledge of dark psychology and manipulation tactics to help other people regain their power, individuality, and confidence. I have experienced the detrimental effects of narcissism, gaslighting, and manipulation firsthand. I know what it's like to feel defeated, isolated, and like you've lost yourself. So, to help you and any victims you may know to protect yourselves and consequently build a strong mental and emotional defense against dark psychology influences, *A Practical Application of Dark Psychology* was born.

Together, we will discover what dark psychology is and how to use it to defend and protect yourself. We will uncover the importance of standing up as a victim and regaining your independence. Through this book and the knowledge and experience I want to share with you, my goal is to help you use dark psychology to *free* yourself and begin the healing journey.

CHAPTER I

WHAT IS DARK PSYCHOLOGY AND WHY YOU NEED IT

"When you make your friend do something against his or her will, it is not called convincing. It is basically called manipulating."
Edward Williams

Dark psychology refers to the darker aspects of human nature and involves people using manipulation, tactics of motivation, and control to get what they want. It's a very controversial topic because it is an extremely powerful tool that can be used for both good and evil. It is important to understand what dark psychology is so that you are able to identify it in your life. For example, the debate between persuasion or manipulation – you may think that someone is simply persuading you, but in reality, you are being manipulated. Persuasion aims to serve, while manipulation intends to hurt. In both cases, the person is attempting to influence another individual; however, persuasion is not dark psychology, and manipulation is. Throughout this book, *dark psychologist* refers to anyone who uses the techniques of dark psychology. This chapter will delve into some of the essential things you need to know about dark psychology.

WHAT IS DARK PSYCHOLOGY?

At its core, dark psychology is understanding and exploiting the weaknesses of human psychology (Mrkonjić, 2022). By understanding how people behave, dark psychology practitioners are able to easily manipulate and control others. Dark psychology is used for various reasons, from getting someone to purchase something they don't need to convincing someone to break the law. Psychotherapists have identified three personality traits that make up the *Dark Triad;* psychopathy, narcissism, and Machiavellianism. These traits are often (but not always) found in dark psychology practitioners or people who exhibit manipulation, callousness, and a lack of empathy, which we will cover in more depth in Chapter 3.

While dark psychology can be used for *dark* purposes, it can also be used for good. For instance, therapists can use the methods of dark psychology to help their patients overcome phobias and fears. In other cases, law officials can use dark psychology techniques to get confessions out of criminals.

WHO USES DARK PSYCHOLOGY AND MANIPULATION

Dark psychology tactics can be used by anyone but are often utilized by people in positions of power to control those "beneath" them. For example, politicians use dark psychology to manipulate the media into showing them off in a positive light. An employer would use dark psychology to keep their employees in line by controlling them. A salesperson employs manipulation tactics to make potential customers buy their products. While these examples show people who would potentially use dark psychology tactics, it is important to remember that anyone can be a target of these techniques.

Although many people consider dark psychology techniques immoral, everyone can benefit from learning about dark psychology. Understanding how these tactics work allows you to defend yourself against being manipulated and controlled. And if you ever find yourself in a situation where you need to use dark psychology, you can be sure that you are using it for good and not evil.

THE AREAS THAT DARK PSYCHOLOGY IS USED IN

Dark psychology tactics differ depending on the situation at hand. Certain forms of manipulation or mind games are better suited for specific outcomes. Some of the basic approaches of dark psychology include using a personal trigger to gain control over a person or exploiting their insecurities to weaken their self-confidence and efficiency. Understanding the dynamics of dark psychology makes it easier to manipulate others more effectively and use their vulnerabilities against them (Sintelly App, 2021).

USING DARK PSYCHOLOGY FOR SOCIAL MANIPULATION

Utilizing dark psychology in a social context means using strategies, procedures, and techniques to influence and control a person to make them do whatever the dark psychologist practitioner wants – this is beneficial for them but damaging to their targets. Many people use the following techniques even if they are unaware of their names; they simply have a natural "knack" for manipulation. Here are a few examples of the tactics employed by dark psychologists in a social situation:

1. Guilt trip power move: with the lack of real power, dark psychologists use a "sympathy play" to make others feel bad and do what they want out of a place of feeling guilty.
2. Social scalper: this tactic involves exaggerating what they've done for others to get more social-exchange credits than what is due. This technique uses the reciprocity principle to get more than what is given.
3. Feminist manipulation: the dark psychologist tells other women to be strong and independent. This makes dating harder for the target and easier for the exploiter.

USING DARK PSYCHOLOGY IN DATING

When it comes to dating and relationships, psychological principles are applied to ensure that dark psychologists' own physical and sexual needs are met at the expense of the person they are dating.

In general (but not always), the dark psychologist is a male that strings a female along without having a proper relationship. This includes pretending to want to settle down but constantly postponing getting serious, as well as lying about aspirations for the future of the relationship. Other tactics could also involve being unfaithful but lying about it – promising commitment but never delivering.

Another common occurrence is *chameleon manipulation,* where the dark psychologist wears the mask of an ideal partner instead of the partner they actually are. They pretend they want the same thing as their partner, which leads to the target lowering their defences, allowing the dark psychologist to get to the "sex part" quicker.

On the other hand, when the dark psychologist is female, they tend to position themselves as a prize that needs to be won. They turn their target down and pretend to have no interest in order to make the victim chase them. This tactic is used to keep the victim interested and attentive, making them more inclined to invest in the relationship. Female dark psychologists also use sex as a manipulation tool to get what they want – given as a reward or retained as a punishment.

USING DARK PSYCHOLOGY IN SEDUCTION

When dark psychology is used in seduction, the psychologist uses the technique of seeking bonds and attachments based on traumatic experiences (instead of mature love) to leverage or create psychological wounds.

A few examples of these seduction tactics include:

1. Regression seduction: this is a form of seduction that mimics mother or father roles.

2. Judge seduction: the dark psychologist conveys themselves as superior and forces the victim to chase them for any form of approval.
3. Traumatic bonding: this tactic involves the dark psychologist making their partner attached to them through physical or emotional abuse.
4. Emotional roller-coaster bonding: the dark psychologist makes their partner attached to them through cycles of fights and reconciliation.
5. Control through personal kinks: this tactic involves the dark psychologist providing sexual satisfaction through fantasies the victim keeps a secret. This results in the dark psychologist being the only person who can sexually satisfy the partner, and they hold the secret over their partner to give them leverage.
6. Love bombing: this is a common method used by psychopaths and involves the dark psychologist making their target feel special and unique through constant attention and admiration.

USING DARK PSYCHOLOGY IN GROUPS

In general, group leaders who utilize dark psychology want to diminish their member's authority while increasing their own leverage and control. To make the group members more dependent on the group, the group leader will use a few dark psychology tactics, including:

1. Making their problems bigger than they are: they make the group members believe that they are needed to solve a problem but cannot do it without the group leader.
2. Mocking, disempowering, or ruling out people who disagree: the dark psychologist group leader will cut out all conflicting opinions. When this is not possible, they will overpower any challenging voices by mocking them, discrediting them, or making them appear deceitful. This

causes other group members to keep quiet out of fear of embarrassment or being viewed as an outcast.

3. Fabricating a big, colossal enemy that can only be conquered as a group: creating an enemy that is too large to take on alone causes the group members to want to seek protection within the group.

USING DARK PSYCHOLOGY IN BUSINESS

Dark psychologists use their tactics in business to manipulate their employees into sacrificing their own needs and self-interest for the sake of the business while accepting a small monetary portion of what they're really worth. These tactics include manipulation mottos; for example, we are a family, employees matter, we can make a difference together, etc. These manipulation techniques get the employees to work in adverse conditions for the sake of the greater good.

USING DARK PSYCHOLOGY IN POLITICS

Politicians use dark psychology in the form of propaganda and political debates that put their opponent's in a bad light, influence their voters and cause the public to abandon individualistic thinking and behavior in favor of the collective. The tactics used for politics can be grouped into two parts; dark psychology during campaigns and once they're in office.

In a democracy, these two phases overlap, but you will still notice an obvious switch from the campaign to the office. Here is a look at the difference:

1. During the campaign, politicians use dark psychology to:

- Make their opponent appear ineffective and unfit.
- Create a sense of hopelessness for the current state of the country.
- Frame themselves as the person to fix the situation.

- Make up an enemy and assure the people that they're the right person to take down that enemy.

2. Once in power, politicians use dark psychology to:

- Reframe the state of affairs as positive.
- Accept credit for the things that are running well.
- Find scapegoats for the things that are going badly.

Government officials are essentially group leaders. In the case of radical governments, they act the same way as the leaders of cults and hate groups. They use principles of dark psychology like:

- Fabricating enemies.
- Increasing group unity through extremist ideals and religious zealots.
- Fueling the fears of the public and framing themselves as the only ones able to tackle the danger.
- Fueling anger as a diversion ploy.

USING DARK PSYCHOLOGY IN WAR

Dark psychology even extends to something as major as war. There are many techniques used, and they seek to instill terror, manipulate the media, frame the enemy as barbaric, and mentally dominate the enemy to negatively impact their fighting ability. Here is a brief look at a few of these tactics:

- **Terror to win without conflict**

One of the biggest dark psychology techniques in war is leading the enemy to surrender without even firing a shot. This can be done by purposefully creating a reputation of ruthless brutality toward anyone who goes against the dark psychologist. Encirclement tactics of superior firepower also cause the enemy to surrender without any action. In an odd way, this form of dark psychology actually saves lives.

- **Psychological warfare**

One of the greatest examples of psychological warfare was the light bomber plane Stuka which had a siren on its nose. This was used to spread fear among ground troops and build an association in the minds of the soldiers between the siren sound and impending chaos and death. Once the troops realized that they couldn't defend themselves from the attack, they retreated.

- **Wartime manipulation**

There are five elements of wartime manipulation

1. Portraying oneself as good or "holy."
2. Framing the enemy as evil, oppressive, and brutal.
3. Making a victory seem easy.
4. Hiding the true monetary cost of war.
5. Hiding the true emotional cost of war.

WHAT BENEFITS CAN YOU EXPECT, IF YOU UNDERSTAND AND APPLY DARK PSYCHOLOGY

Part of understanding and applying dark psychology is accepting that everyone has a dark side (Buffalmano, 2019). When you were little, did the dark scare you? Most people were afraid, and we never really thought to question this fear. It was almost like we were naturally taught to be afraid of the dark because the dark is unknown. But what happened when you turned on the light? You learned that the unknown things weren't that scary and weren't so unknown – they were just a part of the environment around you.

We have been taught to associate darkness with fear and that it's better to keep quiet about our dark thoughts and emotions. Switching the light on our internal shadows is a lot more tricky than flicking a physical light switch, so we avoid it. But this darkness inside has a life of its own which thrives, whether we choose to acknowledge it or not. It is there, and it is powerful. This fear of your dark sides grows as you grow, and with time it becomes your *shadow self*. It is a hidden part of you that influences your decisions more often than you are aware of.

We spend so much time repressing and hiding our shadow self from ourselves and others – the parts of us that we're ashamed to show. But in many ways, hiding this shadow is one of the highest forms of betrayal. By concealing this part of yourself, you are saying that you don't deserve to show your complete self and thereby betray yourself. Embracing your shadow self does not mean that the "evil" side of you is going to come out. The shadow within is not evil; it is simply a normal part of every human being. The shadow can show itself as a weakness or a strength. By becoming aware of your dark side, you allow yourself the opportunity to express strength. On the other hand, ignoring these parts of yourself will always produce a damaging result. The more these dark corners are repressed, the more chance there is of a disorder in your personality that can manifest as anxiety, addiction, failed jobs and relationships, and other self-destructive behaviors.

To embrace your shadow is to shed light on your earliest wounds and give yourself a chance for transformation and healing. However, as long as you choose to suppress the shadow within, the wounds will carry on decaying and leeching poison into your life.

Embracing your shadow self is all about self-awareness.

Here are a few of the benefits of knowing and accepting your dark side:

1. You become more conscious of how criticizing others could actually be a defense mechanism – we accuse others of our own flaws, and often the traits that irritate us in others are things we don't like about ourselves.
2. You are able to understand how your words mask fear, anxiety, envy, and jealousy.

3. You become more in touch with your fears and anxieties, allowing you to handle them better.
4. You gain more clarity on the relationship dynamic you have with other people. This also helps you notice if you are being influenced by a dark psychologist.
5. You are able to fully accept yourself, which is incredibly freeing.
6. You can release all guilt about the dark side of yourself. You will realize that it's not actually as scary and unknown as you once believed. Turning the light on inside means you can use your shadow self for the positive, and you no longer need to feel guilty about your dark thoughts and feelings.

COMMON MYTHS ABOUT DARK PSYCHOLOGY

There are many distorted beliefs regarding what dark psychology is and what it's not. Contrary to popular belief, dark psychology does not mean someone can stealthily control people's minds. It is not the same as brainwashing either. Here are a few common misconceptions about dark psychology (Buffalmano, 2019):

- **Dark psychology is not hypnosis**

Hypnosis may still be an "out there" concept for many people, but it is powerful. Hypnosis involves a series of well-executed commands to gain control over an individual. The person enters a trance-like mental state where they experience increased attention, concentration, and suggestibility. Once the person is engaged in a hypnotic state, they disengage their critical thinking, and their compliance escalates to the point of doing things out of their control.

- **Dark psychology is not neuro-linguistic programming (NLP) or undercover seduction triggers**

Well-design stimuli, for example, an auditory pattern, can change a person's mood and induce a trance-like state which can help with seduction. NLP uses conscious language to bring about changes in a person's thoughts and behavior. However, this is not what dark psychology does.

- **Dark psychology doesn't turn anyone into a cult follower**

There is no doubt that cults and sects are real, and cult leaders do use dark psychology principles to entrap people. However, it is a myth that some could be recruited into a cult and blindly follow it. There is a general rule about manipulation, *"A manipulator's biggest skill is picking targets that are easy to manipulate."* Now that's not to say you should walk around thinking you're unable to be manipulated; it can still happen to anyone. But it does mean that the influence of dark psychology in sects is limited by the victim's own power.

- **Brainwashing**

Dark psychology is not brainwashing. Brainwashing requires complete control over a person and does not work on everyone. It also takes a long time, and the effects of brainwashing tend to dissipate after a while.

- **World domination by a small group of people**

The idea that the Illuminati, the government, the CIA, or any small subset of people can control what every individual thinks and how they behave is because of the power of propaganda and not dark psychology. And while propaganda is powerful, the world is too complex to be completely manipulated by a small group of people in a fancy room.

- **Subliminal manipulation**

Subliminal manipulation is obvious through advertising, but it only works when there are existing associations present in the brain. It is also not possible to change deep-seated ideals and beliefs with subliminal manipulation.

- **Creepy pictures**

Clowns, scary dolls, Halloween costumes, and other "dark" imagery are not dark psychology.

IN SUMMARY

Although dark psychology is a relatively new field of study, it is still effective. While dark psychology can be used for nefarious purposes, it can also be used for good. It is important to understand dark psychology and embrace the dark side of yourself so that you are well-equipped to defend yourself against manipulation, control, and the other techniques accompanying this practice.

In the next chapter, we will take a look at persuasion and how to use it to effectively convince others and get what you want.

CHAPTER 2

THE ART OF PERSUASION – HOW TO GET WHAT YOU WANT

The real persuaders are our appetites, our fears, and above all our vanity. The skillful propagandist stirs and coaches' internal persuaders.
Eric Hoffer

H aving influence is a power – maybe even a superpower. You may be wondering if some people are just born with more natural charm than the rest of us? Possibly. But rather than focusing on what gifts nature did or didn't give you, it's better to study the practice of persuasion and harness influence as a skill to greatly impact your life.

WHAT IS PERSUASION, AND HOW DOES IT WORK?

Persuasion is the process of convincing another person or group to change their point of view, beliefs, and behaviors, follow a specific course of action, say yes to a commitment, or buy a product or service. However, persuasion is different from coercion because the people receiving the message have a choice about whether they want to act on it or not. Despite everything that is known about persuasion, people continue to misunderstand it and fail to make good use of its true nature.

Persuasion is a contronym, a word with two opposite meanings. For some people, persuasion has a negative connotation and is associated with seduction, force, or cajole. For others, persuasion has a positive meaning and is related to encouragement, inspiration, and motivation. Some communication theorists have declared that persuasion is "ethically neutral" – it is neither good nor bad but purely an impartial process (Cherry, 2022).

WHAT ARE SOME EXAMPLES OF PERSUASION?

In your everyday life, there is a chance you could come across various situations where you need to persuade other people or other people attempt to persuade you. Here are a few common examples of persuasion (Indeed Editorial Team, 2021):

1. Media advertisements are a form of persuasion. Marketing professionals use written and visual cues to influence people's buying decisions. Large-scale campaigns also make use of advertising and media to persuade diverse audiences regarding social causes like vaccination drives, sustainability, and cancer awareness.
2. Videos, speeches, and news articles are an example of a speaker using their persuasion skills in action.
3. A salesperson uses their persuasion skills to get people to purchase a product or service or convert a potential customer into a loyal supporter of a specific brand.
4. Teachers, counselors, and mentors persuade their students to engage in their education and make good career choices.
5. Business owners and top executives use persuasion during negotiations and agreements to ensure only the best for their business.

6. Team managers and group leaders use persuasion to motivate their team members to get their work done or work ahead of deadlines.

THE SIX PRINCIPLES OF PERSUASION

The cornerstone of the psychology of persuasion is an established set of six principles. These principles were identified by Robert Cialdini in 1984 and define what makes persuasion influential and successful. The principles – reciprocity, scarcity, authority, consistency, liking, and social proof – are universal, and often a few of these tactics are used simultaneously (Juma, 2015). Mastering these six principles will allow you to maximize your persuasion abilities. However, a word of warning, these skills can be used to control and manipulate others, so don't abuse them.

1. Reciprocity

One of the most basic ways to influence others is to simply give what you want to receive. Doing right by other people is a good way to have the favor returned and get others to do the same for you. Reciprocity is a powerful principle, and there are a couple of ways to use it to your advantage. Giving people small gifts, treating others respectfully, and helping those in need are all ways "win points" with other people. In essence, the reciprocity principle is always helping others and being kind when you have the chance because you never know how it will help you down the line. People also remember small acts of kindness, which will pay off when *you* need a favor.

2. Scarcity

People place more importance on what is not readily available. As things become more rare, they become more valuable. There are a few ways to use the scarcity principle to persuade other people. One method is to make your offers a one-time deal, limited to a set amount of time, or limited to a small supply. This immediately creates a sense of scarcity, and people have more urgency to accept the offer before it runs out. At the same time, how you present these offers is also important. Focusing on *loss language*, or language that describes what the person will miss out on rather than gain, is more powerful. Another method under the scarcity principle is the exclusivity approach, which involves providing access to services, information, or other items to a limited number of people. This creates a sense of exclusiveness and is often viewed as doing a favor for certain people or that those people are valued more than others.

3. Authority

When you are seen as an expert in a certain area, other people will be more likely to defer to you. This is because experts can offer people a solution that would otherwise take a long time to devise themselves. The idea of this principle is to establish your credibility of authority and expertise from the very beginning. People often miss this opportunity because they assume that others will automatically see them as an expert. However, you cannot leave this up for other people to interpret because it will often go unnoticed. There are a few ways to establish yourself with authority. The first method is to make all diplomas, credentials, and awards clearly visible to establish your background, but this may not always be possible or appropriate. Another method is communicating your expertise through short stories or background information during casual conversations. Remember that your experience isn't always known, so be sure to communicate it when you get the chance.

4. Consistency

The consistency principle is centered around the power of active, public, and voluntary commitments. This results in people actually sticking to their word. The first part of this principle involves an active commitment. This refers to something that is written or spoken to other people. Having someone say that they will do something is a start, but when they actively commit to it by telling others about it, they are more likely to follow through in their actions. The second part of the principle is making it public. When people see commitment, it adds account- ability to the statement. Finally, it needs to be voluntary. If someone is forced to make a commitment that they didn't choose, you have accom- plished nothing. So how do you put this principle into play? Once you have persuaded a person to do something, you need to get them to make the commitment to implement the principle of consistency and guarantee that there is a genuine devotion to their words.

5. Liking

People like people who like them. It is a simple yet powerful idea. The liking principle can be used in several ways. The first method is to find common ground with people you meet. If you can connect with them on a more personal level, you have a solid ground to build from. Being observant of people is a good way to pick up on any clues that can lead to this common ground. The second approach is through genuine praise. Compliments and charm go a long way when building positive relationships with others. However, be careful not to go overboard – the key is *authentic praise* and not trying to butter someone up with fabri- cated compliments.

6. Social Proof

This final principle is based on the fact that people rely on social cues from others on how to behave, think, and feel in many situations – and not just any random people, specifically their peers. This is a crucial point and what is known as social proof. For example, hotel towels. A sign that says, "eight out of ten hotel guests choose to reuse their towels," is a lot more effective at persuading than a sign that simply says, "reusing your towel helps save the environment."

So, if you want to influence a particular group of people, you need to get one individual to buy in first. When others see that person taking action or following a new directive, they are more likely to follow along. Having the first people take action unlocks the power of social proof and makes all the difference.

WHAT SKILLS DO YOU NEED TO MAKE YOU MORE PERSUASIVE?

Persuasion skills can be a personality trait or a natural talent. These skills can also be learned and mastered with practice and determination. Here are some essential skills that will help you develop your persuasion abilities (Indeed Editorial Team, 2021):

1. Communication skills
2. Emotional intelligence skills
3. Active listening skills
4. Logical reasoning skill
5. Interpersonal skills
6. Negotiation skills

HOW TO IMPROVE PERSUASION SKILLS?

To be efficient at persuading, you need to expand on and master the skills mentioned above. Here are six ways to master each one of the skills needed for persuasion (Indeed Editorial Team, 2021):

- **Developing your communication skills**

When it comes to persuading others, someone who mumbles or lacks confidence will not be as effective as someone who speaks with intent and certainty. It is important to enunciate and only use non-verbal gestures that are clear to understand. Don't use unnecessarily big words; keep your vocabulary simple and positive. Focus on building integrity and credibility rather than intimidating the listener.

When you share your ideas, be engaging and use a tone that appeals to the person listening. List the positive aspects of your idea and avoid degrading theirs. For example, if you are using persuasion to sell a product, focus on talking about how fantastic your product is instead of the shortcomings of the product they already own.

- **Building emotional intelligence**

When using persuasion, it is important to evaluate the feelings and emotions of the person before you speak to them. With practice, you will be able to respond to scenarios in an appropriate manner and adapt your persuasion methods to the situation you're faced with. While some people may prefer a matter-of-fact attitude and a concise argument, this won't always be the case. Some individuals may demand a more detailed explanation and require you to be more empathetic. Emotional intelligence is an important skill because, with it, you are able to assess a person's mood and willingness to be persuaded and adjust your arguments accordingly.

- **Listening actively**

Active listening means being considerate and respectful when hearing someone's opinion. To build on this skill, you need to develop patience and listen without interrupting. Listening attentively is about giving people time to talk about their viewpoints and allowing them to share their thoughts and feelings in a comprehensive way. When people feel heard, they are automatically more comfortable in the conversation and more likely to trust you. Once you've built that trust, it becomes a lot easier to persuade.

- **Using logic and reasoning to support your arguments**

It is never a good idea to argue from a place that lacks logic. You need to rely on rational thought, reliable facts, and sound reasoning when attempting to persuade people. Gather comprehensive data and give the other person a chance to examine the information, interpret it, and come to their own conclusions. Testimonials and reviews from credible sources are great tools to include when persuading others.

- **Improving your interpersonal skills**

Interpersonal skills relate to your ability to communicate and interact well with others to maintain meaningful relationships. You can develop your interpersonal skills through authenticity, behaving naturally, and being charismatic. Remember that people will notice if your behavior is forced, which reduces your integrity and your chance of persuading them.

- **Mastering the art of negotiation**

When attempting to persuade people to do something, you need to show them the benefits of engaging in what you're recommending. If the benefits match their expectations, they are more likely to be persuaded. To increase your negotiation skills, try to assess a person's expectations and determine their motivation, intent, and reasoning for it. Once you have gauged this, you can make genuine, visible efforts to see if you can meet their expectations.

TRAITS AND BEHAVIORS OF HIGHLY PERSUASIVE PEOPLE

Persuasive people have an uncanny way of enticing you to lean toward their way of thinking. Here are the 15 traits and behaviors that highly persuasive people use to their advantage (Bradberry, 2016):

- **They know their audience entirely**

Persuasive people know their audience thoroughly and use this to communicate with that audience on a level they can relate to. Knowing your audience is essential because it helps you adjust your pitch to the person in front of you. Whether it's taking your assertiveness down a notch when engaging with someone who is shy or irritable or turning it up for the aggressive, high-energy type, everyone is unique, and understanding these subtleties goes a long way in getting them to hear you out.

- **They form a connection**

It's easy to dismiss people trying to persuade you if you are not emotionally invested in them or their argument, and very persuasive people know this. Persuasive people form a connection by showing empathy for your position and making it known that they're on your side. People will be more willing to accept your point of view once they have insight into what type of person you are. For example, the probability of someone hearing you out is a lot higher if you introduce yourself and briefly share your background before attempting to reach an agreement. The key to connection is understanding that the person you are engaging with is human, not an opponent or target. No matter how persuasive your argument is, if you cannot connect on a personal level, the person will likely doubt everything you say.

- **They aren't pushy**

Persuasive people convey their ideas with confidence and assertiveness without being pushy or aggressive. Pushy people will only send others running for the hills. A persuasive person doesn't ask for much, and they don't argue back and forth because they understand that subtlety is what wins people over eventually. If you are inclined to come across as too forceful, focus on remaining confident but calm. If your pitch is solid, people will eventually catch on in time. If you don't give them space, they won't catch on at all.

- **They aren't mousy**

On the other hand, lacking assertion and posing your ideas as questions or as if they require approval makes them appear unreliable, weak, and unconvincing. If you are more on the shy side, place emphasis on presenting your ideas and statements or interesting facts for your audience to ponder. Also, practice removing all qualifiers from your pitch. When you are trying to persuade people, "I think" or "maybe" have no place.

- **They use positive body language**

Being mindful of your actions, words, and tone of voice and keeping them positive will result in your audience engaging with you and opening up to your point of view. Body language, like a passionate tone of voice, using your hands, keeping eye contact, and leaning toward the person you're talking to, are all great forms of positive body language that people use to persuade others. Positive body language helps your audience see you as someone with a valid argument. When it comes to persuasion, the way you say something can often be more important than what you're saying.

- **They are clear and concise**

Persuasive people don't *um and ah*; they are able to deliver their point of view quickly and clearly. When you completely understand what you're talking about, it's exciting and effortless to explain your ideas to people who don't understand. When you are attempting to persuade someone, you need to know your topic so well that you can explain it to a child. If you can deliver your argument effectively to someone without prior knowledge of the subject, you can certainly persuade someone who has an idea of what you're talking about.

- **They are authentic**

Being authentic and sincere are essential to being persuasive. People see right through a fake act and tend to gravitate toward genuine people because they feel they can trust them. The likelihood of someone believing you when they don't know who you really are or how they feel about you is slim. Persuasive people are confident in who they are. By focusing on what you are passionate about and what makes you happy, you automatically become a lot more interesting, and your persuasive power increases. You can't win someone over by pretending to be who you assume they want you to be.

- **They acknowledge your opinion**

One of the greatest persuasion tactics is to concede to the point. By acknowledging that your argument is not flawless, you show people that you are open-minded and willing to adapt. Being open to adjustments and not obstinate about your case shows people that you have their best interests at heart. When engaging with an individual, use phrases like, "I see, that makes a lot of sense," and "I understand where you are coming from." Acknowledging people's opinions shows that you are actively listening to their points of view and that you're not only interested in forcing your opinions on them. Persuasive people do not invalidate others but rather allow people to be entitled to their own opinion.

- **They ask good questions**

Speaking to someone who is only thinking about what they want to say next instead of listening to what you have to say is very off-putting, which is definitely not good when you're trying to persuade someone. A simple way to avoid doing this is by asking questions. People want to know that you're listening to them, and something as easy as a clarification question shows them that you're paying attention and care about what they have to say. Asking meaningful questions is a sure way to gain respect and appreciation.

- **They paint a picture**

Humans are visual creatures and are more likely to be persuaded by an argument with visuals that bring it to life. If you want to be highly persuasive, you need to use this to your advantage and incorporate powerful visual imagery. If actual images are inappropriate or unavailable, you can tell vivid stories to paint a better picture of your idea. Effective stories create relatable images in people's minds that are difficult to forget.

- **They leave a strong first impression**

First impressions are powerful. From the moment someone meets you, they start forming judgments about you. The impression you imprint in the first few seconds of meeting your audience influences their response to any new information they learn about you. Then they spend the rest of the time internally rationalizing their initial reaction. This may sound extremely daunting, but knowing this will allow you to take advantage of that crucial first meeting. A good first impression puts you leaps and bounds ahead in your likability and power to persuade.

- **They know when to step back**

Pressure is persuasion's mortal enemy. When people are forced to agree to something instantly, they are more likely to get their back up and stand by their original viewpoint. Putting someone under pressure will cause them to counter your ideas in favor of their own. If your argument is rooted in reliability and you're confident about it, you shouldn't be scared to back off and give someone time to let your viewpoint sink in. Often, good ideas are challenging to process immediately, so giving someone a bit of space can go a long way in your chance of persuading them.

- **They greet people by name**

Your name is a fundamental part of your identity, and hearing someone use it makes you feel valued. Persuasive people make a habit of remembering people's names so they can use them every time they see them. If you are good with faces but names enter through one ear and exit through the other, have some fun, and make remembering someone's name a brain exercise. When someone introduces themselves, repeat their name aloud, and don't be scared to ask for their name one more time if you forget it right after hearing it. Use the mnemonics (Patterson, 2021) technique and anchor their name to a certain feature. For example, in your mind, a simple "Tim" might become "Tim with the tattoos," or "Kirsty" might become "Kirsty with the crazy hair." Next time you see them, the feature will remind you of their name.

- **They are pleasers**

People who are good at persuading never achieve a minor victory that ultimately results in a larger defeat. They know when and how to be firm but are also continually making sacrifices for their cause. Powerful persuaders are always submitting, always giving ground, and doing favors for others that make them happy. They are in no way pushovers, but they do this because they know that this wins people over in the long run. It's important to remember that it's better to be effective than to be "right."

- **They smile**

It is natural for people to unconsciously mirror the body language of the person they're engaged with. A smile goes a long way in getting someone to like you and believe in you. Smiling during your conversation will make people unconsciously do the same – and feel great as a result. Persuasive people are typically always smiling because they have a real passion for their ideas. This enthusiasm is infectious and leaves people feeling good when they talk to you.

While persuasion is a science, it is also an art. It is a balance between pushing your perspective without being forceful; being assertive but not dismissive. With the right combination, a thorough and persuasive message will help you both personally and professionally. Whether you are trying to persuade your boss to fund your project or convince your toddler to put their shoes on, persuasion is a skill that is instrumental to success in your life.

IN SUMMARY

You may not be born with a natural knack for persuasion, but it is a skill that can be learned and developed. One of the most essential parts of effective persuasion is that people are more prone to be swayed by those they like. Persuasion is ultimately about being true to yourself and confident in your case. Mastering the skills of persuasion will not only make you more successful at getting your own way, but it will likely also improve your life for the better. There's definitely nothing wrong with being helpful and kind – and having that little boost of confidence to help you throughout your life!

In the next chapter, we will take a deeper look into the dark triad of character traits: narcissism, Machiavellianism, and psychopathy – and how they are often connected.

CHAPTER 3

NARCISSISM AND THE DARK TRIAD

Realize that narcissists have an addiction disorder. They are strongly addicted to feeling significant. Like any addict, they will do whatever it takes to get this feeling often. That is why they are manipulative and future fakers. They promise change, but can't deliver if it interferes with their addiction. That is why they secure backup supply.

Shannon L. Alder

The term narcissist is often misused. Narcissism is typically associated with anyone who often talks about themselves or puts a lot of effort into their appearance. However, narcissism goes a lot deeper than situational instances of demanding attention. Someone monopolizing a conversation to talk about their annoying colleague or fitness fad may be a narcissistic tendency. But a true narcissist actually has a personality disorder, which has more traits than just enjoying talking about themselves or posting a dozen selfies.

The word narcissist comes from the mythological figure Narcissus (T. Editors of Encyclopaedia, 2022). He was the son of the nymph

Liriope and the river god Cephissus. Narcissus was distinguished for his beauty and fell in love with his own reflection.

WHAT IS NARCISSISM?

To some degree, narcissism is a personality trait that every one of us possesses. A certain amount of self-centeredness is actually healthy. Research (Lubit, 2002) has shown that it contributes to ambition, confidence, and resilience. But, like with any characteristic, narcissism has a spectrum, and every person falls somewhere along the continuum. For example, someone tweaking their Instagram selfie for the 47th time and still not being happy with the number of likes they're getting is on the low end of the scale, while someone with severe narcissistic tendencies lies on the extreme side of the scale, for example, someone that uses emotionally abusive tactics to shift any blame onto others (Brennan, 2022).

Narcissism is a pathological self-absorption and was first identified as a diagnosable mental disorder by Havelock Ellis, a British physician, in 1898 (Rhodewalt, 2023). If a person is excessively high in narcissism, they have *narcissistic personality disorder* (NPD). However, it is important to keep in mind that not every narcissist has NPD. Because of the spectrum, a person can still have extreme narcissistic tendencies but not be officially diagnosed with the disorder – although that doesn't make them any less toxic.

Narcissism is an extreme form of self-involvement. While everyone may show the occasional traits of narcissistic behavior, a true narcissist ignores the needs of those around them and often disregard other people or their emotions. When you first meet a narcissist, they tend to be very charming and charismatic and don't often show negative behavior immediately, especially in relationships. Narcissists build relationships that fuel their egos and reinforce their beliefs about themselves, even if these relationships are trivial. Narcissists also have a habit of exaggerating their abilities and achievements while undermining those of the people around them. They spend most of their time obsessing over power, success, and aesthetics. Narcissists place themselves on a pedestal above others and believe they are superior to everyone else. However, they also constantly need praise and admiration and react poorly to any form of criticism.

A good example of a narcissistic personality is someone that became my best friend. He frequently fueled my ego and made me feel good about myself. However, it got to the point where he started to follow his compliments with favors, and then the favors turned into demands. He would make me feel bad for not doing what he asked, for example, giving him money when he needed it or even just dropping him off at his parent's house. Because he always used to boost my confidence with compliments and positive talk (especially when I was feeling down), he made me feel like I was a terrible person for not complying with his requests. It was almost like I owed him for spending his precious time to help me out, something any genuine friend would never hold against you.

Narcissistic personality disorder affects up to 6.2% (Kacel et al., 2017) of the population and is slightly more common in men than in women. A person with NPD has an extremely inflated sense of superiority that masks a fragile sense of self-esteem to the point where it interferes with their normal daily functioning. Studies have shown that this is partially due to differences in the brain. People with NPD often have less brain matter in the areas associated with empathy and increased matter in the regions of the brain associated with self-absorbed thinking (Pedersen, 2013).

HOW MANY TYPES OF NARCISSISM ARE THERE?

Research has indicated that there are two key categories of narcissism: adaptive narcissism and maladaptive narcissism. These primarily highlight the difference between the productive and unproductive aspects of narcissism (Telloian, 2021).

1. Adaptive narcissism: this refers to the aspects of narcissism that can potentially be helpful and positive, like

independence, self-confidence, and the ability to celebrate yourself.

2. Maladaptive narcissism: this is associated with the traits that negatively impact how you relate to yourself and others. For example, aggression, entitlement, and the tendency to use other people for personal gain. This is linked to the symptoms of NPD.

Narcissism can then be broken down further into five main categories: overt, covert, antagonistic, communal, and malignant narcissism. These five types of narcissism refer to narcissism under the maladaptive umbrella.

1. Overt narcissism

This type of narcissism is also known as agentic narcissism and grandiose narcissism and is most commonly associated with NPD. A person with overt narcissism will have the following traits:

- Outgoing
- Overbearing
- Arrogant
- Entitled
- Exaggerated self-image
- Constant need for praise
- Competitive
- Exploitative
- Lack of empathy

Research (Zajenkowski & Szymaniak, 2019) has drawn a correlation between overt narcissism and the personality traits of openness and extraversion. It is believed that people with overt narcissism have a higher chance of feeling good about themselves and are less likely to experience emotions like loneliness, anxiety, or sadness. Overt narcissists also tend to overestimate their own intelligence and skills.

. . .

2. **Covert narcissism**

This type of narcissism is also known as closet narcissism or vulnerable narcissism and is the opposite of overt narcissism. Covert narcissists don't fit the common stereotype of a loud and overbearing person. Instead, they have personality traits that include:

- low self-esteem
- higher chance of feeling anxiety, depression, and shame
- introversion
- insecurity or poor self-confidence
- defensiveness
- avoidance
- tendency to play or feel like the victim

While covert narcissists are very self-focused, they also have an internal conflict where they have a deep sense of not being good enough. Someone with this type of narcissism will have a tough time taking criticism and will internalize or take the criticism more harshly than it was intended. Covert narcissism has been linked to high neuroticism and unpleasantness (Miller et al., 2017). Research (Jauk et al., 2017) shows that overt and covert narcissism are not always independent of one another, and an individual with overt narcissism may go through a time where they show more covert narcissism traits.

3. **Antagonistic narcissism**

This type of narcissism branches from overt narcissism and is more focused on competition and rivalry. Some of the traits of an antagonistic narcissist include:

- arrogance
- taking advantage of others
- constantly competing with others

- disagreeability or proneness to arguing

Studies (Zeigler-Hillb et al., 2017) have shown that people with antagonistic narcissism are less likely to forgive people. They also have higher levels of distrust. (Zeigler-Hillb et al., 2017)

4. Communal narcissism

This type of narcissism is another form of overt narcissism and often contradicts antagonistic narcissism. Communal narcissists value equality and justice and see themselves as unselfish. However, research (Zeigler-Hillb et al., 2017) shows that there is a gap between what they believe and the way they act. A person with this type of narcissism will have the following traits:

- easily morally outraged
- believe they are empathetic and generous
- respond strongly to things they see as unfair

So what differentiates this communal narcissism and legitimate concern for the well-being of others? The answer is that people with communal narcissism place great value on social power and self-importance. They want to be praised and admired for their moral code. For example, a communal narcissist would be a person who pretentiously views themselves as "the most helpful person they know," "the most caring person in their social circle," and "extraordinarily trustworthy."

5. Malignant narcissism

Malignant narcissism is a highly abusive form of narcissistic personality disorder. Someone with this type of narcissism will have a very strong need for admiration and to be superior to others. In addition, they also have the following traits:

- vindictiveness

- sadism and cruelty
- aggression when interacting with other people
- paranoia and an intensified worry about possible threats

Individuals with malignant narcissism also share similar traits with antisocial personality disorder (Pedersen, 2021), meaning they are more likely to fall into substance abuse or commit criminal acts. A study (Lenzenweger et al., 2018) involving people with borderline personality disorder and those with malignant narcissism showed that people with malignant narcissism had a more difficult time reducing their anxiety and gaining a better ability to function in normal scenarios.

Unfortunately, treating narcissism is challenging because many people living with NPD don't necessarily feel the need to change. However, living with narcissism has its own mental health effects, like depression, anxiety, and substance abuse. And sometimes, these effects will result in the person reaching out for help. It is important to understand the various types of narcissism so that you are able to identify these people in your own life and protect yourself using the methods we will discuss in Chapter 4.

WHAT IS THE DARK TRIAD?

The *dark triad* sounds like a horror story starring a secret society of some sort. *But* it's actually the term for the terrifying trio of terrible traits that some people have. The dark triad theory was coined by two researchers, Delroy L. Paulhus and Kevin M. Williams, in 2002. It refers to the three distinct but intertwined negative personality types.

These include:

1. Narcissism: the personality disorder that is defined as a pattern of self-centered, arrogant thinking and behavior with a lack of empathy and complete disregard for other people. This superiority often masks a deep sense of inadequacy.

2. Machiavellianism (Towler, 2020): the use of skillful but often misleading methods that deceive people in order to win power or control. Machiavellianism is defined as extreme manipulation and the willingness to deceive others to get what they want.

3. Clinical psychopathy (Neumann, 2016): is characterized by constant antisocial behavior, little to no empathy and remorse, and a lack of emotional sensitivity. People with psychopathy tendencies are likely to be impulsive and engage in dangerous behavior.

People with the dark triad personality type have been associated with tendencies toward criminal activity and violence. However, even when they don't slip into these extremes, this trio has an undeniable willingness to exploit anyone to get what they want and experience very little regret when they cause harm to other people. They are deceitful, manipulative, self-serving, and aggressive.

Understanding the dark triad traits (Loggins, 2022)

The dark triad traits are typically linked to negative human behaviors. In non-clinical terms, these personality types are displayed by people that are commonly regarded as antisocial. Below we will look at narcissism, Machiavellianism, and psychopathy and how they relate to the dark triad in more detail.

- **Trait one: Narcissism**

Narcissism is the most commonly misdiagnosed of the three dark triad traits. As we discussed above, narcissism runs deeper than someone who occasionally shows selfish tendencies. A true narcissist is self-absorbed and entitled to the point of ignoring the needs of others around them. While many narcissists are simply annoying, malignant narcissists relate to the dark triad through their emotionally or physically abusive tendencies when they are not given the admiration and special treatment they believe they deserve.

- **Trait two: Machiavellianism**

This personality trait is based on the political philosophy of the 16th Century writer Niccolò Machiavelli. Machiavellianism is very closely linked to high intelligence and describes a manipulative person who deceives and tricks others to achieve their goals. Although Machiavellianism is seen as cunningness and the ability to use manipulation, people with this personality trait may get to the point where they use whatever means necessary to gain power and control. The line between Machiavellianism and psychopathy is often blurred.

- **Trait three: Clinical Psychopathy**

Like narcissism, psychopathy is a term inappropriately thrown around to describe people who don't fully exhibit the traits of a clinical psychopath. A true psychopath is an individual that displays antisocial behavior, like weakened impulse control and a lack of empathy and remorse. It is important to mention that these are not once-off occurrences but a continuous theme in the psychopath's life. For a true psychopath, impulsive tendencies and a lack of empathy form the foundation and are not an exception to their behavior. A true clinical psychopath's behavior permeates almost every area of their life. Psychopathy is considered to be the darkest trait of the dark triad, especially because psychopaths typically cause more harm to others than narcissists or people with Machiavellianism.

A narcissist, a Machiavellian, and a psychopath are all standup comedians in a show. The narcissist thinks that they got the most people laughing, the psychopath doesn't care, and it's actually the Machiavellian that got the loudest applause but at the detriment of the other two.

THE DARK TRIAD STUDY

Humor is a fundamental facet of personality and forms a multi-dimensional construct of who a person is. The participants of this study filled out a questionnaire known as the *Short Dark Triad*, a standard measure of dark personality traits. The participants also completed a scientific survey known as the *Comic Style Markers*, which is an assessment of eight different comic styles. These comic styles can be categorized as lighter or darker styles of humor and include fun, humor, wit, nonsense, irony, satire, sarcasm, and cynicism. The lighter styles of humor include fun, humor, wit, and nonsense, and are more positive styles of humor related to benign behaviors, cognition, and goals. Darker humor includes satire, irony, sarcasm, and cynicism and is a negative style of humor that is typically based on ridicule and mockery. These traits are generally associated with poor mental well-being and tenuous relationships (Duradonib et al., 2022).

The researchers of the study found that the darker styles of humor were positively linked with two of the three dark triad traits, Machiavellianism and psychopathy, but narcissists gravitated more towards lighter humor.

Narcissism has a significant link with wit. This is because narcissistic people often use more positive humor as a way to boost their own reputation when interacting with other people. Narcissists use wit to impress and be admired by others. They shy away from the darker styles, with the exception of satire, because they want to be liked by those around them.

Machiavellianism was linked to greater use of irony and cynicism. Machiavellians are devious and intimidating and therefore use humor as a way to manipulate other people. They use aggressive humor to directly belittle others and do this by highlighting other people's weaknesses without damaging their own social reputation. Using irony allows people high in Machiavellianism to make fun of other people without being too blunt.

Psychopathy showed the strongest link to mockery styles of humor like sarcasm, satire, and cynicism. These correlations are based on the fact that traits like lack of empathy, antisociality, aggression, and egocentrism all characterize psychopathy. Psychopaths use aggressive humor to manipulate and belittle others while not considering the feelings of the people around them because of their deficits in emotional functioning.

HOW TO TELL IF SOMEONE HAS DARK TRIAD TRAITS

The devious nature of the dark triad personality is intrinsically tricky to identify. Many people who have this trio of traits are master manipulators and exceptional liars who are accomplished in telling people what they want to hear. It can be tough to diagnose someone high in dark triad traits, and without a proper evaluation, there is no definite way to know. However, if an individual is a repetitive liar, shows little empathy, and manipulates or bullies others to achieve their own agenda, there is a chance they are high in one or more of the dark triad traits.

The following four behaviors are some more signs that someone has dark triad traits (Booth, 2022).

- **They cannot sustain long-term relationships**

Individuals with dark triad traits have a tough time maintaining long-term relationships. This doesn't only refer to romantic partners but also family, friends, and work colleagues. They have a prominent pattern of failed relationships in their lives where they have cut ties with significant people.

- **They have a history of being a "victim"**

People with the dark triad personality are experts in the narcissist cycle of gaslighting and abuse. When they are questioned or challenged, they quickly reverse the situation and play the victim. According to a study published in Sage Journals (Green & Charles, 2019), aggressive and violent behavior is commonly triggered when a person with narcissistic tendencies feels threatened or fears abandonment.

- **Their stories are inconsistent and contradictory**

While individuals with the dark triad traits are masters at manipulating circumstances for their own benefit, over time, they lose track of all their lies. The so-called facts and background details of their lives are erratic and often have gaps in the story.

- **They have a chronic need to be fulfilled**

People with the dark triad personality always have to have their needs met at the expense of those around them. They are constantly looking for some sort of fulfillment, and in the interim, they play the victim, express their disappointment, and are never truly satisfied.

If you suspect someone has the traits from the dark triad, it is best to stay away from them whenever possible. They will leave you feeling emotionally, physically, or even financially depleted. They are entitled, devious, vindictive, and emotionally cold, so it is exceptionally difficult and draining to maintain a healthy relationship with them.

WHAT IS THE LIGHT TRIAD?

On the opposite side of the personality spectrum, there is a *light triad* – faith in humanity, humanism, and Kantianism. These three traits describe a loving, compassionate nature, in contrast to the callous, cynical nature described by the dark triad traits.

Here is a brief look at each light triad trait (Allen, 2022):

- **Faith in humanity**

This trait is the belief that there is fundamental goodness in the core of every person. People who have faith in humanity are naturally trusting, quick to forgive, and always see the best in others.

- **Humanism**

This is the belief that every person is important and deserving of dignity. Humanists stand for the development of a more humane, compassionate, and democratic society using pragmatic ethics based on human reason.

- **Kantianism**

Kantians care about authenticity and don't believe in using other people for their own agenda. Kantianism believes that people need to be treated as "ends themselves" rather than as a means to an end.

IN SUMMARY

Research on the dark triad is always evolving. Many researchers believe that narcissism, Machiavellianism, and psychopathy are three distinct traits with overlapping characteristics. However, other people believe that the overlap points to an underlying personality construct that has yet to be fully understood. Personality traits are complex, but in general, there are three unifying perceptions to watch out for: anger, selfishness, and disagreeableness. When all three of these traits are present, so too is the dark triad.

The next chapter deals with identifying a narcissist, as well as how to deal with them and leave them if that is an option.

YOUR CHANCE TO HELP
SOMEONE FREE THEMSELVES
FROM A NARCISSIST

We hope you are enjoying reading our book about defending yourself against a narcissist using the teachings of dark psychology. Our goal is to provide practical and effective strategies for those who are struggling with narcissistic abuse. We believe that everyone deserves to live in a healthy and respectful relationship, free from emotional manipulation and psychological abuse.

If you found our book helpful and informative, we would be truly grateful if you could leave a review on Amazon. Your feedback is essential to our work and helps other readers find the resources they need to protect themselves from narcissistic abuse.

By leaving a review, you are not only helping others who are suffering from narcissistic abuse but also supporting our work. As an independent author and publisher, we rely on the support of our readers to reach a wider audience and make a positive impact on people's lives.

To leave a review, simply go to the Amazon page of our book and click on the "Write a customer review" button or scan the QR-code below. You can choose to rate our book and write a short or long review, depending on your preference. Your review will be visible to millions of Amazon customers and can have a significant impact on our book's visibility and success.

We understand that leaving a review takes time and effort, and we are truly grateful for your support. Thank you for taking the time to read our book and for considering leaving a review on Amazon. We hope that our book has provided you with the knowledge, skills, and confidence you need to protect yourself from narcissistic abuse.

CHAPTER 4

IDENTIFYING AND DEALING WITH A NARCISSIST

I don't care what you think unless it is about me.
Kurt Cobain

A narcissist will do anything to maintain their appearance, but once you know what to look out for, you are able to unmask them, and then you can decide how to proceed. This chapter will look at why narcissists get their hooks in so deep and how to leave one to start a new life.

WHY IS LIFE WITH A NARCISSIST SO HARD?

The personality traits connected to narcissism can make life for the partner of a narcissist rather difficult. People on the extreme end of the narcissism spectrum can be demanding, entitled, and selfish. Here are a few reasons why life is so hard with a narcissist.

- **They have little empathy and lots of aggression (Vergin, 2019)**

One of the prominent characteristics of a narcissist is their lack of empathy. They aren't interested in hearing the opinions of others, rarely listen, and prefer to talk about themselves in every situation. If you have a terrible day, they aren't going to be the one who listens intently and provides comfort. Narcissists also get very aggressive when their viewpoints are challenged or when they feel like you are confronting them.

- **It's a bottomless pit (Vergin, 2019)**

Dealing with a narcissist negatively impacts a person's self-esteem. Before you even know it, they make you feel worthless and miserable – and no longer like the person you used to be. People with NPD are like a bottomless pit. Deep down, they have no internal worth, so they are always seeking external validation. Most narcissists mask the fact that they have very fragile self-esteem and demand endless admiration and praise.

- **They shirk their chores and responsibilities (Pedersen, 2022)**

When it comes to housework and chores, narcissism can manifest in one of three ways. The narcissist can either avoid their chores completely because they believe they are above doing housework and errands. Or, they will do lots of housework just to make you feel perpetually indebted to them. The third way is to constantly criticize you in everything they do, making you too scared to even wipe the counter in front of them. Regardless of how it manifests, the underlying traits of narcissism are always a lack of empathy, an intense need for admiration, and an over-inflated sense of self. In other words, their actions are probably driven by self-serving purposes and a need for power, and your feelings will likely not be considered.

Here are some of the ways that narcissism can manifest in responsibility:

1. Because of their lack of empathy, it doesn't matter if you have worked two jobs or are down with the flu; if the laundry isn't done, it's affecting their life, and you will hear all about it.

2. They have an unrealistic sense of entitlement, so even just suggesting that they pack the dishes away in a different way to save space will likely result in them getting aggressive and pointing out everything you do "wrong."

3. They constantly need to be the center of attention, so if they do housework or run an errand, it's not for the sake of getting it done. They do it to be praised for being an amazing and helpful person. If they happen to tidy up the kitchen before you get home and you don't notice it immediately, they will likely bring it up in an aggressive manner.

4. Narcissists have a habit of making people feel worthless and will use every opportunity possible to criticize you. If you get up to clean, they might accuse you of making them look bad. If they start cleaning and you are in the middle of something else, they might accuse you of making them do everything.

5. Narcissists tend to gaslight others. They might insist that they took the trash out the night before when you know for a fact that you took it. But the narcissist will keep insisting that it was them until you feel like you've lost your mind and second-guess yourself.

- **They use the silent treatment (Bonchay, 2016)**

The silent treatment is a very common method of emotional abuse utilized by narcissists when all their other schemes have been tried and failed. Narcissists employ silent treatment as a way to gain control in their relationships. It's also a way for them to avoid discussing important issues and how they manage to get out of taking responsibility for anything they've done wrong. They use the silent treatment to make you feel invalidated and insignificant. The narcissist will likely also blow the entire situation out of proportion and demand a perfectly delivered apology. If they don't deem the apology as good enough, they will extend the "punishment." By doing this, they reiterate their dominance and support their inflated importance.

- **They have zero appreciation (Newman, 2015)**

When dealing with a narcissist, it is generally easier to let them get their own way than to bring it up and have an argument. For example, if you agreed to meet for lunch at 1pm, they might show up whenever they want, and you could even be waiting for hours without so much as an apology. However, if the tables were turned and you were late to lunch, you would be asking for forgiveness until the end of time. The victim doesn't want to come across as petty, so they let the actions of the narcissist slide, which means that the narcissist always wins. Conforming to a narcissist is the reason they keep you around. However, these efforts are never shown any form of appreciation. It doesn't matter what you do or how much time, energy, or money you put in; you are only giving them something they believe they are entitled to.

- **You lose your sense of self (Newman, 2015)**

When you make any decisions, your mind probably wonders what the narcissist would say. You don't try a particular product because the narcissist said it's a waste of money. You don't sign up for the class you've wanted to attend because the narcissist says it's a waste of time. You buy a specific phone because the narcissist said it's the best. Their judging eye and harsh opinion always echo in your mind even when they are not around. But what about what you want? Do you know what still makes you happy? If the narcissist wasn't in your life, what phone would you have bought? What movie would you go and see in the cinema? What would you cook for yourself to eat? You need to ask yourself what you truly want, without the influence of the narcissist, and start putting those needs first.

When we accommodate the egotism of a narcissist, we are only affirming that our needs don't matter as much as theirs do. We don't like to believe that we have let our guard down to the point that we are being manipulated – and we don't want to believe that the narcissist is a lost cause. But if you started putting the effort into yourself that you put into making a narcissist happy, you could become the self-confident person the narcissist pretends to be.

HOW TO KNOW IF SOMEONE IS A NARCISSIST

We have all tossed around the term narcissist to describe someone self-absorbed, especially when it comes to relationships of all kinds – familial, romantic, workplace, or even friends. Perhaps you've used the word to describe an ex who always put their own needs and desires above yours, or maybe it was a boss who constantly cut you off in meetings and took credit for all your accomplishments. However, here are some of the signs that you're dealing with a narcissist. According to the American Psychiatric Association, a true narcissist will display 5 or more of the following characteristics.

- **They monopolize conversation**

Dominating a conversation is the most obvious trait. Narcissists talk over or interrupt others to make the conversation about themselves or express their views. They also have a habit of ignoring what other people say or only responding with trivial comments before steering the conversation back to being about them. These traits come partly from the following:

- An extreme need for admiration
- A sense of entitlement
- A lack of empathy
- An excessive need to be the center of attention.

- **They flaunt rules or social conventions**

One of the more unruly signs that someone is a narcissist is their need to defy rules or traditions, even if there are consequences. Narcissists might feel offended or seek special treatment when they can't bypass the system. They feel like the rules exist for other people but not for them. Examples of these traits include:

- Infringing on traffic laws
- Stealing supplies from work
- Cutting in front of people in queues

- **They are fixated on appearance**

Narcissists spend hours in front of a mirror every day, constantly fixing or adjusting how they look. They are also more ready to discuss the appearances of others and may directly belittle people by criticizing their body shape, haircut, clothes, and facial features. In addition to their obsession with appearance, narcissists also focus on establishing "unforgettable" impressions on others. They inflate or even makeup stories that make them look more important. Narcissists also place importance on the fact that their lives appear perfect. They don't only need to keep up with the Joneses; they need to surpass them.

- **They are envious**

While it's normal for everyone to feel jealous of others at some point in their life, narcissists become completely consumed with envy. They strongly believe that other people are envious of them and use this as a way to get closer to affluent and high-status people. In the workplace, a narcissist's envy causes them to downplay or even steal their colleague's work. They also feel like someone that is doing better than them owes them a break.

- **They have a complete disregard for other people**

Narcissists are not afraid to manipulate others to get what they want. They form intense emotional relationships with friends or family and use that connection to boost their self-importance and benefit themselves.

- **They need an enormous amount of praise**

Narcissists expect admiration everywhere they go. They also expect praise and special treatment from others, even when it's unwarranted. If the compliments don't come naturally, they put themselves in the way of them. This is commonly referred to as fishing for compliments – they will do anything to validate their importance. If they are not admired often enough, they feel slighted, which pushes them to get more compliments. Unfortunately, the slightest threat to their self-image or hint of criticism could unhinge them. If they are unable to get the praise they want, the narcissist often resorts to other – often harmful and sometimes dangerous – tactics to get what they feel they deserve. If the narcissist receives criticism, the situation often implodes.

- **It's never their fault**

Shaming and blaming are two methods narcissists use to manipulate others and exert control. They always shame their victim, and if the victim somehow upsets the balance of power, the narcissist does whatever it takes to reclaim control. They achieve this power by:

- Being disrespectful
- Belittling a person
- Hiding behind cruel jokes
- Criticizing
- Sabotaging

Covert narcissists tend to blame everyone else for their actions and flaws. It is never the narcissist's fault, and they can never accept responsibility for themselves – they rarely ever see the role they have to play in a negative situation.

- **They fear abandonment**

Mental health experts believe that narcissists demonstrate these traits because they fear abandonment. However, most of the time, it's the narcissist that abandons others. In their mind, it's a case of leaving before being left. However, this only results in a vicious cycle of breaking up and making up that only hurts the victim more in the long run as they forget who they are and become entirely dependent on the narcissist.

- **They live in a fantasy world**

Narcissists often have delusions of grandeur. They fabricate grandiose fantasies about their amazing life and success and expect other people to take part in and confirm these fantasies. A narcissist's delusions stretch far and wide and might include the following:

- Being more beautiful and talented
- Being smarter and richer
- Being superior

To support these fantasies, narcissists will construct stories about events that never took place. If the event did occur, they exaggerate the details to make it seem bigger or better than it was. In a narcissist's world, they mingle with only the best, and fans fall at their feet. If someone brings up their idealistic sense of superiority, the narcissist lashes out to protect their false self.

- **There are always strings attached**

People who know the ways of a narcissist know that gifts and favors come with strings attached. Narcissists use unsolicited gifts and acts of service to manipulate their victims into getting what they want. They always ensure that the victim knows who the gift is from and will collect their collateral at a later stage. Narcissists give only to create loyalty, which ensures that no one ever leaves them. Sometimes, a narcissist gives so much that it makes a person become dependent on them, and then there really is no safe way out.

DEALING WITH A NARCISSIST

Confronting a narcissist is rarely ever the best course of action. Narcissists don't often recognize that they have a problem, and confronting them will only result in them trying to maintain the upper hand. Instead of focusing on "fixing" a person with narcissistic personality disorder, focus on your own behaviors and well-being. This includes setting boundaries and building stronger relationships with a support system of friends, family, and professionals.

Here are some helpful ways to deal with a narcissist (Pietrangelo & Link, 2018):

- **Educate yourself**

Narcissists are often charming and likable when you first meet them, making it easy to overlook their other toxic behaviors. However, familiarizing yourself with the traits of NPD is important, so they are easier to spot. Educating yourself on NPD will also give you a better understanding of the person's strengths and weaknesses so that you are ready for any challenges along the way. Learning about narcissists is also the first step in accepting them for who they are and establishing more realistic hopes about your relationship with them.

- **Understand the abuse cycle (Smith, 2022)**

The narcissistic abuse cycle involves four phases: feeling threatened, abusing others, playing the victim, and feeling empowered. Learning to identify what phase the narcissist is in will allow you to stop the cycle.

. . .

Phase one: Feeling Threatened

Something upsets the narcissist, and they feel threatened. It could be anything from embarrassment in a social setting to feelings of neglect, disrespect, or rejection. Aware of the potential threat, the victim of the abuse gets nervous and walks on eggshells around the narcissist. In general, narcissists frequently get upset over the same underlying issue and tend to obsess over the threat repeatedly.

Phase two: Abuses Others

The narcissist exhibits some sort of abusive behavior – either verbal, physical, sexual, mental, financial, or emotional. The abuse is tailored to each individual victim in their area of weakness, especially if that area is one of the narcissist's strengths. The abuse can last anywhere from minutes to hours. Typically the victim defensively fights back.

Phase three: Playing the Victim

This is where the switch occurs. The narcissist flips the table and begins playing the victim by bringing up past defensive behaviors that the victim exhibited, as if the victim initiated the abuse. Because the victim has feelings of guilt and remorse, they are manipulated into believing this twisted perception and try to rescue the narcissist. This might include giving in to what the narcissist wants, accepting responsibility for something that wasn't their fault, appeasing the narcissist to keep the peace, and agreeing to the narcissistic lies.

Phase four: Feeling Empowered

Once the victim has given in, the narcissist regains their power. This is all the narcissist needs to declare their superiority. The victim has unknowingly fed the narcissist's ego, making it stronger and brasher. However, every narcissist has an Achilles heel, and the dominance they feel now will only last until something else threatens their ego again.

Once you understand the cycle, you can get away at any point. You can develop strategies for future confrontations and have an escape plan in place. The cycle does not need to continue.

1. Work on your self-esteem

Practicing positive self-talk, prioritizing self-care, and finding a solid support system are all ways to build your self-esteem and develop resilience. Healthy self-esteem will make it easier to cope with the potentially harmful behaviors you could encounter in a relationship with a narcissist. Self-confidence will also make it easier to be assertive, advocate for yourself, and set clear boundaries.

2. Speak up for yourself

Sometimes it might feel easier to pick your battles and simply walk away in certain scenarios. But it is very dependent on the relationship. For example, dealing with a partner, parent, or boss will require a different approach than dealing with a child, sibling, or co-worker. If you feel your boundaries have been disrespected when communicating with a narcissist, do your best to stay calm and confident – you don't want to react badly, get flustered, or show annoyance. If the narcissist is someone you'd like to keep in your life, you owe it to yourself to speak up (calmly and gently). Remain direct and consistent with what is inappropriate and how you expect to be treated. However, just prepare yourself that it may be challenging for the narcissist to understand and empathize with your feelings.

3. Set clear boundaries

Instead of trying to change a narcissist, it's best to set clear boundaries about unacceptable behaviors from the beginning. You need to constantly enforce your boundaries if they are crossed. Don't allow the narcissist to walk all over you. Idle threats and ultimatums are not enough – you must ensure that you are being taken seriously. For example, you have a work colleague with NPD who parks skew across your parking spot. Begin by firmly asking them to park straight, so you have enough space to park your car. Then, state the consequences if they don't respect your space or boundaries. Such as, "If I can't park my car in my own allocated parking, I will have to have your car towed." The key is to follow through on this and call the towing company if it happens again.

4. **Practice skills that help you keep your cool**

Practicing yoga, meditation, or deep breathing will help you stay calm and prevent a negative reaction when interacting with a narcissist.

5. **Find a support system**

If you can't or don't want to avoid the narcissist, build up a strong support system of friends, family, and professionals. Spending too much time in a dysfunctional relationship with someone with NPD will leave you emotionally drained, so it's important to get out – rekindle old friendships and nurture new ones. If your social circle is on the small side, try taking a class to explore a new hobby where you could meet like-minded people. Find something to do that allows you to meet more people that rejuvenate you.

6. **Insist on immediate action, not just empty promises**

Narcissists are good at making promises but bad at keeping them. They might promise to stop doing the thing you hate or promise to generally do better. Although direct confrontation is not recommended, calmly and lovingly let them know that you'll fulfill their requests once they have fulfilled yours. Stay consistent and follow through on your end of the deal as long as they do the same.

. . .

7. Understand that a narcissist may need professional help

Narcissists typically have other disorders like substance abuse, mental health, and personality disorders. It's this disorder that may cause them to seek help. And remember, while narcissism is a diagnosable personality disorder, it does not excuse abusive or harmful behavior.

8. Recognize when you need help

Maintaining a relationship with a narcissist takes its toll on your own physical, mental, and emotional health. If you feel anxious, depressed, have unexplained physical ailments, or feel negatively impacted by the relationship with this challenging person, it is crucial to see a healthcare practitioner. Once you have had a checkup, you can engage with other mental health professionals and support groups. Reach out to your family and friends; there is no need to go it alone.

LEAVING A NARCISSIST

The common traits of NPD make sustaining a healthy relationship undeniably difficult unless the narcissist is very aware of their behavior and has the ability to control it. Unfortunately, this is very rare for most people. So, if you are at the end of your wits and can't carry on, you are not alone. When you cannot make it work despite your best efforts, or you're just tired of trying, it's time to learn how to leave the narcissist (Firestone, 2022).

WHY LEAVING A NARCISSIST IS SO HARD

To an outsider, leaving a toxic relationship seems like an easy decision. After all, who wants to be with someone arrogant, needy, manipulative, and emotionally cold? Of course, every situation is unique, and there is no easy answer to this question. However, there are some common themes that everyone who wants to leave a narcissist struggles with (Firestone, 2022).

1. Fear of being alone: narcissists are masters at destroying your friendships and relationships with family members, so the choice to leave a narcissist may result in being alone for a while.
2. Fear of retaliation: narcissists create a deep sense of fear and anxiety in their partner's life. Sometimes emotional, physical, or sexual abuse may be present in the relationship, making this fear even worse. You may be afraid of the narcissist's revenge or explosive reaction to rejection.
3. Holding out hope for change: You may believe that you can fix the narcissist and that if you stay, things will get better.
4. Cognitive dissonance: this way of thinking causes you to lie to yourself about the reality of the situation to rationalize the conflict that arises when you stay in a situation that doesn't match the way you know it should be.
5. Feeling needed: narcissists have a habit of making you feel needed. Because narcissism is often built on deep-seated insecurity, when you get emotionally close to a narcissist, you may catch a glimpse of this and feel like the narcissist needs you.
6. Fear of losing yourself: narcissists take up so much of a person's time and energy, so leaving them can cause you to feel like you are giving up a part of yourself if you leave. You may feel like you will be lost without them.
7. Feeling worthless: everyone possesses an inner critic that tells us that we are undesirable or unworthy. Being with a narcissist makes you feel good in some ways because it "feels good" that a person with such a high opinion of themselves chose you. On the flip side, a narcissist may also make you feel tiny by belittling and putting you down whenever they feel challenged or you fail to meet their need for admiration. Or they may knock your confidence by ignoring you and making you feel unworthy. Being treated like this supports your already negative attitude toward yourself, making it even harder to be alone.

HOW TO LEAVE A NARCISSIST

It's important to remember that leaving a narcissist is unlike leaving a "normal" person. Narcissists are good at twisting words, guilt-tripping, and using manipulation tactics to keep you in the relationship. If you want to leave a narcissist, the following tips can help (BetterHelp Editorial Team, 2022).

- **Be prepared before you leave**

Getting prepared with aspects of your life, like how to move your belongings and where you'll live once you leave, can be helpful before you even say a word to your partner. This allows you to leave quickly when the time comes. It's also important to have any necessary legal and financial documents in order, as well as any keys you may need. Consulting with an attorney or accountant before you announce you are leaving may also make the split as clean as possible.

- **Don't try and have a conversation about it**

When the time comes to break the news, it needs to be done as quickly as possible. Let the narcissist know that you're leaving and share any other relevant details, but leave it at that. Keep your answers short, and do your best to keep your emotions out of it. As soon as you get into a discussion about the relationship, there's a good chance that the narcissist will draw you back in. Once you decide to leave and have everything in place, make it a quick goodbye, and don't wait around to hear what they have to say. If you are worried about it being difficult to leave quickly, ask someone from your support group to be there with you. The narcissist may be less likely to manipulate you when there is another person around to see it.

- **Stick to a no-contact rule, or include a third party**

Once you've left, avoid all contact with the narcissist. If you have to be in contact, have a third party person involved in the communication.

- **Prepare yourself for retaliation**

The narcissist will retaliate out of anger and hurt. However, they may also move on more quickly from the relationship than you can. Do your best to anticipate their retaliation and prepare yourself for it – be ready for verbal and emotional abuse. Change your passwords and PINs if the narcissist had access to them to stop them from doing something like draining your bank account. It's also a good idea to block them from any social media accounts.

- **Pack up all reminders of your relationship**

Cutting all ties is one of the best ways to move forward, and this includes getting rid of any reminders. Unfortunately, if you have children together, the situation gets more complicated, but look for ways to cut down on the things that remind you of the narcissist.

- **Build a support system**

It may feel overwhelming and lonely if you've been isolated from friends or family and no longer have close relationships with them. But just remember that there's a good chance these people still care about you and want to support you. Work on nurturing these relationships again and surround yourself with a solid support system. If there is no one you can reach out to on a personal level, think about joining a support group of people that have been through it already. Hearing from people who have experienced this situation that can offer support and advice is still a good idea, even if you have close friends and family.

- **Choose your battles carefully if there are children involved**

Co-parenting can be a nightmare when your ex is a narcissist. However, it helps to remember that your situation is unique and doesn't need to look like all the other co-parenting relationships around you. If you have joint custody and joint expenses, there will be some challenging conversations that the narcissist will want to control. It's in these moments that you need to pick your battles. Think about what things are worth fighting for and what things are a big deal.

- **Seek professional help**

Speaking to a therapist can be extremely helpful when you're in a relationship with a narcissist or once you've left one. After being with a narcissist, it can be hard to trust other people, and there will be many difficult emotions to deal with. Having a professional that you can speak to will help with the healing process.

ALLOW YOURSELF TIME TO HEAL

It takes time to heal from any broken relationship, so be kind to yourself. Allow yourself time to navigate the grieving process, and remember that grieving is not only for people that have passed but for anyone or anything you have lost. Take time to discover yourself again, and don't rush into any new relationships. Work on building yourself up one step at a time and lean on your support group. It will take time to recover from leaving a narcissist, and the process may be tough, but it is also the first step towards a completely new and improved life.

IN SUMMARY

Dealing with a narcissist can be incredibly challenging. If possible, the best course of action is to steer clear. If that's not an option, you need to understand narcissists and their abuse cycles so that you know how to handle any situation you're faced with. Speak up for yourself, set clear boundaries, enforce your boundaries, and have a strong support network you can rely on when you need it.

In the next chapter, we will dive into gaslighting and why it is such an effective tool for narcissists and manipulative people.

CHAPTER 5

GASLIGHTING: A NARCISSIST'S STRONGEST TOOL

Gaslighting is the systematic attempt by one person to erode another person's reality by telling them that what they are experiencing isn't so – and, the gradual giving up on the part of the other person.
Dr. Robin Stern

Gaslighting is a word that is often thrown around freely, but genuine gaslighting is a serious and intentional form of abuse. In simple terms, gaslighting makes someone question their own reality. It includes a range of tactics like lying, minimizing, distracting, blaming, and denying. It is not always easy to identify because it begins subtly and usually accompanies other forms of abuse.

People who struggle with low self-esteem, anxiety, depression, or a history of trauma tend to be more prone to being gaslit. They have a tough time trusting themselves or have been told by other people that they cannot trust themselves, making them more susceptible to manipulation and gaslighting techniques. However, even though they are more at risk, gaslighting can happen to anyone.

GASLIGHTING: WHAT IT IS AND WHAT IT'S NOT

Gaslighting is a method of psychological manipulation where the abuser (known as the gaslighter) attempts to plant insecurity and confusion in their victim's mind. The goal of a gaslighter is to obtain power and control over someone else by using methods that distort reality and force the victim to doubt their own judgment and natural instinct. The term "gaslighting" comes from the play Angel Street, which Alfred Hitchcock later used as inspiration for the film *Gaslight*. This movie is all about a man trying to convince his wife that she is going crazy in order to steal from her. There is a specific scene where he turns on the attic lights to look for her jewelry collection, which causes the gas lights to dim downstairs. He constantly tells her that it's all in her imagination, and she slowly begins to question her own recollections of reality (DiGiulio, 2018).

Gaslighting commonly occurs in abusive relationships and is closely linked to other forms of emotional and physical abuse. While gaslighting happens more frequently in romantic relationships, it can also take place within family, friend, or workplace relationships. An example of a familial gaslighting relationship is a mother that constantly disapproves of her daughter's decisions to the point that the daughter questions anything she suspects her mother would disagree with. The mother may or may not be consciously aware of her desire to control her daughter's every move, but by being overly judgmental, she's doing so. Another case of non-romantic gaslighting is silent sabotaging in the workplace. A gaslighting boss or coworker might try to sabotage another employee's reputation by jeopardizing their work. For example, they might promise to send over vital documents only to never send them. Or, they might "forget" to invite the employee to a meeting, only to scold them later for not showing up (DiGiulio, 2018).

However, recognizing that you or someone you care about might be the victim of gaslighting is not always as simple as it seems because it starts off in very subtle ways. It often involves two people (or a group of people) who seem to care about one another a lot. Gaslighting tends to start with seemingly small offenses, but the problem is that eventually, these more-or-less insignificant scenarios cause you to question your own judgment and reality. This is all because of the deliberate intent of someone else, and once it starts, it snowballs. Gaslighting causes you to end up in a cycle of not navigating your daily life in a way where you are clear-minded, able to focus, make sound decisions, and have a sense of well-being. No matter whether the gaslighting is happening in a marriage, between a leader and their constituency, or in another type of relationship, it is important to be aware of the red flags – which is the first step to escaping the abusive situation. You need to be wary of gaslighting when you begin to question yourself a lot (DiGiulio, 2018).

GASLIGHTING VS. MANIPULATION

Manipulation is a crucial part of gaslighting; however, there is a *fine line* between manipulation and gaslighting. Influence and manipulation are common marketing and sales tactics to get people to buy a product or service. Every single person is capable of manipulation, and we learn it from a young age – think about a small kid who learns manipulation by getting something from one parent when the other says no. But, manipulation becomes a serious problem when the influencing turns into a sequence of behaviors where the only intent is to gain power and control over someone else. This is where the line blurs into gaslighting. The biggest difference between manipulation and gaslighting is intent. The more common types of manipulation are about getting our own way and what we want (Gillihan, 2018). On the other hand, gaslighting is all about controlling another person through consistent behavior patterns.

GASLIGHTING VS. NARCISSISM (OR SIMPLY BEING A JERK)

Gaslighting is a part of a narcissistic personality, but narcissistic personality disorder is also multi-dimensional and consists of many other pieces (Gillihan, 2018). Gaslighting and narcissism are more related to sociopathic behavior than just being a jerk. If someone is just an idiot, it's easy to brush them off with, "Whatever – they're just a jerk." But gaslighting is more than an annoyance, it gets under your skin and makes you question yourself. Jerks typically just repel people, but gaslighters are dangerous because they both repel and hook you simultaneously.

GASLIGHTING VS. A HEALTHY ROMANTIC ATTACHMENT

Gaslighters are skilled at attracting unsuspecting people, which can look a lot like the charming and positive signs of strong romantic potential at first. However, there are some other red flags to be aware of if you know what you're looking for. If the person speaks poorly about their parents or ex-partners by calling them derogatory names, that is a warning. Another sign is if they completely overdo it by telling you how great you are and how you are the best thing that's ever happened to them before you're even through your meal at the restaurant. While a small percentage of first dates are love at first sight, it doesn't happen often. So if you are being loved bombed from the get-go, it's a definite red flag. Of course, it feels good to be told how wonderful you are, but if it crosses the line from a normal compliment to being bombarded with sweet talk, it is merely a tactic the gaslighter is using to suck you in (Gillihan, 2018).

GASLIGHTING VS. OCCASIONAL BAD BEHAVIOR

The difference between gaslighting and the occasional bad behavior is the consistent pattern. When a series of these bad behaviors are strung together consistently, you have a gaslighter. It is different from someone just having a bad day or lying once in a while. Gaslighting is an amalgam of behaviors that are very indicative of abusive behavior when exhibited together (Gillihan, 2018).

TYPICAL SCENARIOS WHERE A NARCISSIST WOULD USE GASLIGHTING

Narcissism and gaslighting are partners in crime. Narcissists use gaslighting to gain control over their victims. It is difficult for people to leave these abusive relationships because the victim often doesn't realize that they are dealing with the manipulation tactics of a narcissistic gaslighter until it's a little too late. To understand what it's like to be the victim of a gaslighting narcissist, imagine being stuck in a room filled with smoke. The room is foggy. The air is so gray that you cannot see anything more than a few inches in front of you. The room stinks, your eyes are burning, you cannot breathe, and you feel suffocated. The exit door is wide open, and you can easily walk out. But you don't because it's not just your vision that is clouded; it's also your mind. Being the victim of narsissistic gaslighter erodes your self-esteem and ability to make decisions. This means that making the decision to leave seems almost impossible, even though you really want to. Your learned helplessness keeps you trapped in the room, unable to see a way out (Shafir, 2022).

A narcissist may use many gaslighting tactics, but they all involve misleading, emotionally manipulating, or distorting the facts. This is generally a deliberate action with the goal of causing the victim to question themselves and is common in people with NPD.

Here are some typical scenarios where a narcissist uses gaslighting. (Sadaf & Bose, 2022)

- **Citing your previous mistakes**

This technique involves challenging your credibility by pointing out any previous mistakes you've made. You know that person that constantly brings up your faults from the past, especially the ones you're ashamed of? They are doing this to undermine your confidence in yourself while providing a (distorted) reason for why they can't trust you.

- **Pulling the *you're-crazy-card***

Accusing someone of being mentally or emotionally unstable is a common tactic used by narcissists. They might outright accuse you of being insane or mentally ill, or it might be more suggestive, like, "Maybe you're imagining things in your head, but that's not what happened." If you get upset or angry, they use this reaction as further "evidence" that you are unstable.

- **Questioning your memory**

Another common gaslighting example is for the narcissist to question your memory and imply you're misremembering the facts. Common examples of this are calling you "mixed up or confused." Alternatively, the narcissist might twist it around and say something like, "I have no idea what you're talking about," or "I don't remember that."

- **Calling you over-sensitive**

This is one of the cruelest gaslighting phrases. You are not oversensitive. The narcissist is just cold-hearted and *insensitive*. By accusing you of being too sensitive, the narcissist suggests that your emotions prevent you from seeing the situation clearly. By saying things like, "You take things too personally" or "You are too emotional," they can avoid being held accountable for their hurtful words or actions by making it seem like it's your fault for being upset.

- **Shifting blame to avoid accountability**

Blame-shifting is a common narcissistic gaslighter tactic. When a narcissist is caught out on something, they will twist and distort the scenario to make it look like your fault. They will always find someone else to take the fall for their lies and behavior. For example, they may accuse you or someone else of doing something wrong and "provoking them" instead of owning up to their actions.

- **Accusing you of having no sense of humor**

Another one of the nasty statements that gaslighting narcissists use is, "Learn to take a joke." They crack jokes at your expense, and when you're offended, they accuse you of having little to no sense of humor. It is never a joke if the purpose is to offend or hurt you, even if it's said nonchalantly. When you confront them about their rude jokes upsetting you, they will likely make fun of you with statements like, "Oh, don't make a mountain out of a molehill," or "I was just joking. There's no need to get so worked up." These are all ways that gaslighters with NPD prove they're right and make you question yourself.

- **Love bombing**

"I'm doing this because I love you" is a common phrase that narcissistic gaslighters use, and this tactic is known as love bombing. Narcissists always use love as a defense to manipulate you into believing them. Some of the other common statements look like, "Trust me, I know what's best for you," or "You need to trust my actions." These phrases are a way for the narcissist to shower you with fake love, affection, concern, and intimacy. They use your innermost desires, secrets, and insecurities to exploit you mentally. Another way gaslighting narcissists use love is whenever you challenge them. They will accuse you of not loving or trusting them to guilt you into backing down.

- **Constant criticism**

Gaslighting narcissists use constant criticism to cause you to question yourself, regardless of how good you are at something or what your strengths are. They will criticize your life and career choices, the way you dress, what you eat, and other lifestyle choices. This might look like, "You have no control when it comes to food" or "You are not wife material." Another method of criticism is to compare you to other people in ways that make you feel inadequate. For example, saying something like, "You should ask "so-and-so" for help because they're a lot better at it than you are." This relentless criticism eventually destroys your sense of self-worth and self-esteem.

- **Pretending to have allies**

Narcissist gaslighters often form alliances with other people to attack and discredit a person or pretend that others agree with them even if they don't. This triangulation scheme is designed to make you feel isolated while causing you to doubt yourself. Narcissists use this tactic by claiming that "everyone" or specific people have spoken negatively behind your back to make you feel even more alone.

- **Feigning concern for your well-being**

Another gaslighting tactic that narcissists use is pretending to care about you as a back-handed way of suggesting you're crazy or unstable. Feigned concern is a passive-aggressive technique that appears to be empathetic but is actually designed to undermine someone's credibility. For example, repeatedly asking if you're feeling okay or telling other people that they're worried about you. They also use this method to seem like the "good guy" in every situation by pretending they are the only one who really cares about you and how other people have been talking negatively about you.

- **Using your own words against you**

Gaslighting narcissists use your own words against you by taking them out of context or manipulating their meaning. They weaponize things you've said in the past to imply that you're contradicting yourself or being a hypocrite. This may look like, "You were the one who suggested...." or "But you said...."

- **Stonewalling to end a discussion they can't win**

When a narcissist feels like they're about to "lose" an argument, they often shut down and stonewall, refusing to continue the discussion. This is an extremely frustrating pattern that prevents you from ever being able to make a point or resolve a misunderstanding. Examples of stonewalling are saying, "I'm not discussing this with you anymore," or declaring, "This conversation is over."

WHY IS GASLIGHTING SO DANGEROUS FOR VICTIMS?

Just like with other forms of abuse, the gaslighter (or abuser) seems stable, confident, sincere, and empathetic, which makes the gaslighting dangerous and tough to spot. At the start of the relationship, the gaslighter will reel the victim in with love, charm, and affection. Eventually, they'll begin to pit you against the people you once loved and trusted, forcing you to rely solely on them as your source of trust and comfort. The gaslighter will constantly put you down and disregard your experiences as if they never happened. When you start doubting the gaslighter or the relationship, the gaslighter will use a tactic known as "hoovering." They will suck you back into the relationship by charming you, making false promises, and making you doubt yourself. You become incapable of remembering what is true or not and begin to question your own sense of reality. In extreme cases of gaslighting, the victim is unable to believe themselves and are only able to believe the gaslighter. When you are the victim of gaslighting, your self-confidence diminishes completely (Lane, 2022).

Gaslighting is a terrible form of psychological abuse that makes you doubt your own reality, feelings, memory, and even sanity. When you doubt your view of reality and you don't know if you are sane, you become *insane* to the degree that you are completely detached from reality. The levels of sanity and insanity vary in different areas of life because everyone has certain blind spots, lapses, or lack of knowledge in some regard. However, if you are intentionally and repeatedly made to doubt your accurate thoughts, feelings, values, motives, and perceptions, it damages or even destroys you as a person. Doubting your sanity and becoming detached from reality causes an inability to accurately process certain aspects of reality. The gaslighter keeps you questioning your perceptions, the truth, and yourself.

SIGNS OF GASLIGHTING

Being a victim of gaslighting causes anxiety, depression, and other mental health concerns like addiction and suicidal thoughts. For this reason, it is essential to recognize if you're being gaslit. Ask yourself if any of these statements ring true (Gordon, 2022).

1. **You doubt yourself and reality:** you try and convince yourself that the way you're being treated isn't that bad or that you're being too sensitive.
2. **You question your perceptions and judgment:** you are scared to speak up or express your emotions. You have learned that voicing your opinion only makes you feel more miserable in the end, so you keep quiet instead.
3. **You feel insecure and vulnerable:** you often feel like you're walking on eggshells around your family member, colleague, friend, or partner. You always feel on edge and lack self-confidence.
4. **You feel isolated and powerless:** you are convinced that other people just think you're unstable, strange, or insane, just like the gaslighter says you are. This makes you feel lonely and trapped.
5. **You question whether you're what they say you are:** the gaslighter's words make you feel like you're wrong, inadequate, unintelligent, or insane, and you often find yourself repeating these statements to yourself.
6. **You are disappointed in yourself:** you are disappointed in the person you've become. For example, if you used to be strong and assertive, you might feel saddened that you have become weak and passive.
7. **You feel confused:** apart from your distorted reality, the behavior of the person gaslighting you is the most confusing

because they are completely different people when you're in public together or alone with them.

8. **You worry that you're too sensitive:** the gaslighter minimizes hurtful statements or actions by saying things like, "I'm only joking," or "You need to toughen up." This makes you concerned that you're just too sensitive and can't take a "joke."

9. **You have a sense of impending doom:** whenever you are around the gaslighter, you feel like something horrible is going to happen. You might often feel threatened, uneasy, or highly strung without knowing why.

10. **You apologize a lot:** you always feel the need to apologize for what you do or who you are.

11. **You feel inadequate:** you constantly feel like you are never enough. You are always trying to live up to the expectations of other people, even if they are unreasonable.

12. **You second-guess yourself:** you constantly wonder if you remember the accurate details of the past. You may have even stopped sharing what you remember out of fear that you're wrong.

13. **You assume that people are disappointed in you:** you always apologize for everything you do based on the assumption that you're letting other people down or you somehow always make a mistake.

14. **You wonder what is wrong with you:** you wonder if there is something fundamentally wrong with you and even worry that you're not mentally well.

15. **You struggle to make decisions because you don't trust yourself:** you would rather allow someone else to make decisions for you and avoid making decisions altogether because you don't trust your ability to decide on something.

If you identify with any of these gaslighting signs, it is imperative that you seek professional help immediately. If left unaddressed, gaslighting will take a huge toll on your emotional, mental, and even physical health.

WHAT TO DO WHEN YOU THINK SOMEBODY IS GASLIGHTING YOU

Knowing how to deal with a gaslighter and what to do when you think somebody is gaslighting you can help you navigate this web of confusion and find yourself again. Here are eight tips for responding to gaslighting and taking back control (Raypole, 2022):

1. **Recognize it as gaslighting**

Determining if you're the victim of gaslighting can be challenging because these behaviors often start off subtly. However, true gaslighting develops into a repetitive pattern of manipulation. The gaslighter's goal is to make you doubt yourself and rely on their version of reality.

It is likely gaslighting if:

- Their behavior happens consistently, repetitively, and across various situations.
- Their behavior makes you doubt yourself.
- Their behavior negatively impacts your feelings of self-worth.

Common gaslighting phrases include:

- "You're making that up."
- "That never happened."
- "You're being so dramatic."
- "You're being paranoid."
- "You're just delusional."
- "Everyone agrees with me."
- "If you loved me, you would...."
- "You're too sensitive."

- "You are just insecure."
- "I never said that."
- "I did that because I love you."
- "You don't really feel that way."
- "You always blow things out of proportion."
- "I'm just joking. You have no sense of humor."

When considering whether someone is gaslighting you, take your feelings into account and not just their actions. For example, gaslighting often leads you to:

- Doubt and question yourself.
- Wonder if you're too sensitive.
- Apologize often.
- Have difficulty making decisions.
- Feel anxious, confused, unhappy, and not like your normal self.
- Avoid loved ones because you don't know how to explain what's going on.

2. Take some space from the situation

You likely feel many strong emotions when dealing with gaslighting, like sadness, anxiety, worry, fear, anger, and frustration. All of your feelings are completely valid, but do your best not to let them guide your reactions. As difficult as it may be, it is important to remain calm so that you can navigate the situation more effectively. Your instincts will cause you to deny what the gaslighter is saying, especially because it's not true. However, they probably won't back down, and your outburst will only encourage more manipulation from their side. Staying calm will also help you focus on what is real, making it less likely that their distorted version of the truth will sway your confidence in yourself. To distance yourself physically, tell the gaslighter you are taking a break and will revisit the topic later. Go for a walk or get some fresh air to help you clear your mind and refocus. If you are unable to physically leave, try breathing exercises, grounding yourself with an object or visualization, slowly counting to ten, or repeating an affirming mantra.

3. Collect evidence

Questioning everything you say, do, or remember is the primary goal of the gaslighter. One way to collect proof is to document conversations and interactions between you and the gaslighter. When they deny a conversation or event ever happened, you can go back to your evidence and check the truth for yourself. Here are a few ideas for documenting interactions:

- Take screenshots of texts and emails
- Take photos of anything that's been damaged
- Note the dates and times of your conversations
- When possible, use direct quotes to summarize your conversations
- Use your phone to record interactions (you may not legally be able to use these recordings, but it is still evidence to use in your defense).

Confronting a gaslighter directly is not always a safe option, but having evidence is very helpful toward restoring your peace of mind and giving you confidence in your recollections of exchanges and events.

To help yourself stay grounded in your own truth, it can also be helpful to journal about your own day-to-day experiences. Keep a record of what is happening in your life, and get into the habit of reviewing these writings often. A journal is a great way to keep track of what is happening and will help you feel confident in yourself and about what you know to be true. When you know the truth, you won't doubt yourself, and this alone will boost your confidence and make it easier to handle the gaslighting in the future.

4. Speak up for yourself

You need to advocate for yourself. Gaslighting works because it confuses you and knocks your confidence. If you show that the behavior doesn't affect you, the gaslighter might decide it isn't worth it. In addition to lies and manipulation, gaslighting also involves criticism. Calling them out calmingly and assertively shows the gaslighter that you will not tolerate their behavior. The gaslighter might disguise their insults as jokes or back-handed compliments. In these situations, ask them to explain the joke as if you don't understand it – this will make them realize that these strategies won't work on you. If a coworker makes a snide comment implying you don't do your fair share around the office, you could respond with something like, "Actually, I've already completed my tasks for the week. We can go over those now if you like."

5. Stand firm in your truth

Everyone recalls things a little differently than how they happened on occasion, and you might find yourself wondering, "What if it did happen the way they said it did?"

It's important not to give into the urge of questioning yourself – the gaslighter wants you to doubt reality. The objective of gaslighting is to have the victim question their perception. To combat this, stand strong in your truth. That means believing in yourself, your thoughts and emotions, and what you know to be true. It means owning your perception. Standing firm in your truth sounds like, "I know what I saw," or "I know what I feel, don't tell me I don't."

You know what happened, so repeat it confidently and calmly. Present any evidence you have as well. However, be prepared that this still might not make the gaslighter back down. If they continue to challenge you, don't be afraid to leave the conversation. Arguing will only draw you in further and leave you feeling frustrated, making you more susceptible to manipulation. By refusing to argue, you are protecting yourself and keeping control of the situation. You could say something like, "It seems like we remember things differently, but I'm not going to argue about it." Avoid any further debate by changing the subject or leaving the room.

. . .

6. Focus on self-care

Dealing with gaslighting may drain you both mentally and physically. To help reduce the negative impacts of experiencing gaslighting, focus on self-care activities. A gaslighter will attempt to make you feel undeserving of self-care or label these practices as indulgent or lazy. However, it is essential to look after your needs despite this.

Try some of these self-care strategies to improve your well-being:

- Spend time with loved ones
- Incorporate positive self-talk into your daily routine through affirmations and mantras
- Make time for hobbies and things you enjoy
- Try yoga or meditation
- Keep a journal to help you sort through your feelings
- Make time to get physically active as an outlet to release tension and stress

Self-care may also include some introspection and taking a closer look at whether the relationship is something you want to continue.

7. Get others involved and increase your support network

Psychological isolation and emotional dependency can be one of the goals of the gaslighter, especially if they have narcissistic personality disorder. You might be worried that talking to other people will lead to unnecessary complications. However, it is important to get insight and support from the people you trust when dealing with a gaslighter. When you reach out to your support system to share your reality – what is happening, what you know, what you have witnessed and experienced – you are integrating this truth further into your mind. The longer you stay quiet and downplay your reality, the more likely that seed of doubt will grow over time. It is important to have external validation from your support system to build your inner confidence. You reduce the emotional and psychological hold a gaslighter has over you when you share your truth with safe people. If the gaslighting is happening at work or in other social situations, avoid meeting with the gaslighter alone when possible. It is best to limit your contact with them altogether, but if you have to meet with them, bring along someone neutral and trustworthy to listen in on the conversation. They are not there to take sides but to merely observe what is happening. A gaslighter will have a harder time trying to manipulate more than one person.

8. Seek professional support

Gaslighting is serious and often accompanies other forms of abuse. It is important to seek professional support, even if you feel like you've got a handle on the situation. Seeking professional help will equip you with the tools and strength you need to deal with the gaslighter in your life. They are also essential for dealing with any damage the gaslighter has already done so you can find and love yourself again.

IN SUMMARY

Gaslighting is not an accident or a result of poor communication. It does not happen because someone is confused or in a bad mood – more often than not, it is intentional behavior. Gaslighting is a form of psychological abuse that is made up of repetitive behaviors. Gaslighting diminishes your self-confidence and keeps you questioning the truth, reality, and yourself. You become incapable of trusting your own intuition and are completely vulnerable to the gaslighter. Recognizing the signs of gaslighting in your life is crucial so that you can distance or protect yourself from people who use this abusive, controlling, toxic behavior.

The next chapter will cover identifying and effectively dealing with chronic liars.

CHAPTER 6

HOW TO IDENTIFY AND PROTECT YOURSELF FROM CHRONIC LIARS

When you're a liar, a person of low moral fortitude, really any explanation you need to be true can be true. Especially if you're smart enough. You can figure out a way to justify anything.
Samuel Witwer

I f you're a human, you've probably told a lie at some point in your life. The truth is everyone lies once in a while. However, the frequency and severity of lying differs from person to person. There is a big difference between someone telling an "innocent lie" and someone that is a chronic liar. It is important to understand the psychology behind lying so that you are able to protect yourself from liars looking to harm you.

REASONS FOR TELLING LIES

According to a study (Docan-Morgan, 2021) with 632 participants, 25 percent of the participants lied more than twice a day. Participants in the top one percent of liars in the study told an average of 17 lies a day.

The study also found that 90 percent of the lies told were small white lies, like telling someone that you love the gift they got you when you really don't. Apart from studying how often someone lied, the research also looked at why they were lying. The responses were broken down into ten different categories, as seen below.

1. **To avoid situations** – People often lie to avoid doing something they don't want to do, like making up an excuse as to why you can't go to a party you're not really keen on. People use lying as a tool to avoid situations and people they don't want to be involved with.

2. **To lighten the mood** – Most people enjoy a harmless prank, and one way to lighten the mood or to get a prank going is to tell a lie.

3. **To protect themselves** – Sometimes people get asked a personal question they don't feel like answering, for example, a stranger in the grocery store asking for your name. You might lie in this situation by giving a fake name to protect yourself.

4. **To protect someone else** – People don't only lie to protect themselves but to protect others as well. For example, has someone ever told you a secret you had to keep to yourself? If you were able to keep the secret, there is a chance that you may have had to lie to someone else at one point or another to keep that information private and protect the other person.

5. **To get others to like them** – A common reason for lying is to impress others. People might stretch the truth to sound more accomplished or increase their popularity.

6. **To gain personal benefits** – Sometimes people lie to benefit themselves and improve their situation in life. For example, lying on a resume to get a better-paying job that can help them improve their skills and provide for their family.

7. **To gain benefits for others** – Lying isn't always selfish, and people often lie for the benefit of their loved ones. For

example, leaving a fake review on your friend's product on their website to help them sell more of it.

8. **To hurt others** – Of course, lying has an ugly side where the liar actually wants to hurt your feelings. People use lying to gain control over a situation or another person; in this case, lying is a tool used to persuade and manipulate others.

9. **To cover up previous lies** – Lies have a way of getting bigger over time, and this snowball effect happens because when one lie is told, more are needed to support or cover up the initial lie.

10. **To tell their side of the story** – In some instances, a person might lie and not even be aware of it because it doesn't seem like a lie to them. For example, telling a story from their point of view to share how specific events were experienced by them. The story might be slightly exaggerated or vary in some ways from someone else's account of the same experience.

VERBAL HINTS OF A LIAR

In general, most people show a few verbal signs that they are lying. For example, you might notice a change in their tone or pick up that something feels *off* in their stories. While there is no definite way to know exactly when someone is being dishonest, there are some verbal hints you can listen for that might raise a red flag (Harris, 2022).

- **Filler words**

For some people, lying takes a lot of mental effort. This causes them to use word fillers, resulting in sentences that don't flow smoothly and stories that don't completely make sense. Filler words, such as *uh, like, er,* and *um,* often slip out when someone is lying because they need to take frequent pauses to consider what words they're going to use next. However, just because someone says *um* a lot doesn't necessarily mean they're lying. Filler words are also called habit words because they're often used unconsciously. If you know the person well and they don't normally use filler words, the sudden use of *uh* and *er* could be an indication that they're lying.

- **They cut out contractions**

In normal conversation, contractions are used to shorten the sentence. For example, using "haven't" instead of "have not." Someone telling a lie might not use contractions when they're talking and rather use the full words instead. Cutting out contractions works similarly to filler words because it allows the person more time to process which direction their lie needs to head in.

- **They pause frequently**

Sometimes the liar will pause often during their conversation. It's normal for people to pause to catch their breath or keep their train of thought, but someone that is lying will pause for longer and more frequently. However, some people can also lie without needing to pause, especially if they've rehearsed the lie ahead of time.

- **They repeat or rephrase the question**

Another way for someone that's lying to buy time is to repeat something they've been asked or something they've already been told. For example, if you ask someone why their car was at the park on a specific day, they might reply, "My car was where? At the park? My car?" as a way to delay and come up with an excuse. Some people may also ask you to repeat the question even though you know they heard you properly the first time. These are all stall tactics to give them more time to formulate a lie.

- **Their pitch changes**

The tone of someone's voice might change when they're lying. Pay close attention to the rise or fall of the person's pitch the next time you think they're telling tall tales. Studies (Streeter et al., 1977) have shown that it's actually common for a liar's pitch to change when they're being dishonest. This is often a result of the person feeling anxious that they're going to get caught lying, and this heightened state causes their voice to strain.

- **They get defensive**

Someone that is lying might become verbally defensive if they're accused of being dishonest. They might unwaveringly deny the accusation or even try and make the person feel embarrassed for calling them a liar. For example, the liar might say something like, "How dare you accuse me?" or "How could you think I would ever lie?" When someone is telling the truth and is accused of lying, they will likely get defensive but will provide more detail about the topic. On the other hand, a liar will just deny it, and instead of offering more detail, they will get aggressive.

- **They change the subject**

A person may change the subject to distract you from the lie. It may be because they've already told a lie and are trying to avoid further follow-up questions. Or, they've left something out of the story, so they turn your attention to a different topic. When you notice this deviation, it could be a sign that you're being lied to. If you're suspicious, continue to ask questions and look for details that don't add up.

NON-VERBAL HINTS OF A LIAR

Sometimes it's easy to spot when someone is lying because of their constant pausing or extravagant stories. However, gauging a person's verbal cues is not the only way to detect a lie. Non-verbal hints can be very revealing in terms of whether someone is lying or not. Here are a few common signs to look out for (Jalili, 2018):

- **Hand gestures**

Someone that is lying tends to use gestures with their hands after they have spoken, as opposed to before or during a conversation. This is because their mind is too preoccupied with making up a story, assessing whether they're convincing others of their lie, and adding more to the story if necessary. A study (2015) examined 120 media clips of high-stake court cases to understand how people behave when lying versus telling the truth. The study found that liars are more likely to gesture with both hands compared to people telling the truth. When people are dishonest, they also tend to face their palms away from you. This is an unconscious signal that they're withholding information, emotion, or outright lying.

- **Fidgeting**

Rocking back and forth, rubbing the fingers, shuffling the feet, and cocking the head to the side can also be signs of deception. This is a result of fluctuations in the autonomic nervous system. When people are nervous, these fluctuations cause them to feel tingles or itches in their body which causes them to fidget.

- **Eye contact**

Someone that is lying might look away or stare at a crucial moment. This is because they're moving their eyes around, thinking about what to say next. It is common for people to break eye contact and look away for brief moments when they're lying, but another sign is for the liar to unwaveringly stare straight at the people they're lying to.

- **Rolling lips**

Rolling the lips backward to the point where they nearly disappear could be a sign of lying or withholding information. People who lie tend to purse their lips when asked questions. This is an instinctive reflex that they don't want to talk.

- **Change in complexion**

It is common for someone telling a lie to have a change in complexion. This could either include going as white as a ghost or getting very flustered and red.

- **Dryness or sweating**

Changes in the autonomic nervous system can trigger sweating in the T-area of the face when someone is lying. On the other hand, the person might experience dryness where they blink excessively, lick or bite their lip, or swallow hard.

- **A change in volume**

People who lie tend to raise their voices to make themselves appear more assertive. In other cases, it could be because they're getting defensive.

PATHOLOGICAL LIARS

It's normal for everyone to tell an occasional white lie, and lying is a tool we use to achieve a goal. However, some people make lying a bad habit and could develop a compulsive lying disorder. Pathological lying is different from the occasional lie and even different from patterns of dishonesty you might see in someone trying to hide a bad habit like infidelity. A pathological liar is a chronic liar, also known as a sociopath. Psychiatrists have recognized pathological lying as a form of behavior that's been around for hundreds of years. It's also known as "mythomania" or "pseudologia fantastica." A pathological liar will lie for no reason at all and do so very believably. The urge to lie is compulsive, and their lies are extensive and elaborate. They often can't control the impulse to fabricate stories, even if it causes them harm, like losing a job or ruining a relationship. Pathological liars are great at lying in all circumstances and often lie just to see if they can trick someone – this is effortless for them because they have no empathy for other people. This form of lying isn't listed as an official diagnosis in the psychiatric guide-book, but it is a very real and troubling condition.

Here are the four main behaviors psychologists use to determine if someone is a pathological liar (Brennan, 2021):

1. **Excessive lying** – Pathological liars lie more than anyone else. They fabricate stories that sound believable enough to get accepted by other people. They then have to add more tall tales to back up the original dishonesty. The lies they tell can also be eccentric and easily invalidated. For example, they might falsely claim to have won a prize or say that a still-living friend has died.

2. **Lying without good reason** – The lies that pathological liars spew differ from the lies "normal" people tell because there is no reason for them. Most people will tell a lie for one of the ten reasons we covered above, but pathological liars have no clear motive. They tell stories that don't necessarily always benefit them and may even harm them when the truth surfaces.

3. **Long-term problem** – Pathological lying is a pattern that takes place over years. It typically begins when the person is young and carries on indefinitely in all areas of their life. Their dishonesty is likely the one thing people remember most about them.

4. **No other mental illness** – A pathological liar might have other mental conditions like anxiety or depression, but that is not the cause of their lying. Pathological lying is a condition on its own, not a symptom of something else.

HOW TO DEAL WITH A NARCISSISTIC LIAR

Narcissistic liars come in various forms, and it's often tricky to tell if someone is just self-absorbed and telling tall tales or if they have no basis in reality and are trying to deceive you with their lies (Singh, 2021).

Who Is a Narcissistic Liar?

A narcissistic liar is someone that uses lying as a tool to get what they want. They are typically charming and persuasive people, but their primary goal is always self-gratification. They use lying to present themselves in a certain light and truly believe they can get away with it. Narcissistic liars are also skilled at rationalizing their behavior, which is one of the reasons they're able to lie so convincingly. Another reason they're so good at lying is that they lack empathy and don't have the same emotional connection to other people that most of us do. Narcissistic liars will say anything to elevate themselves, regardless of the truth or how it impacts others.

Types of Narcissistic Lies

Narcissists use dishonesty to boost their grandiosity and self-esteem. They might exaggerate the truth or outright lie about aspects of their life so that things appear better than they might be. Narcissistic liars have no problem crossing limits or using extreme measures to serve their intent or purpose. They also use lying to distort facts to make others look bad while making themselves look superior, which is called projection. This distortion of reality also takes the form of lying about things that have never actually happened, giving false impressions through body language, placing blame on other people, or being incapable of seeing that they've hurt someone else.

Examples Of Narcissistic Lies

Some common examples of narcissistic lies include:

- Lying about their qualifications to get a position they want.
- Making up stories that make them look good at the expense of other people's feelings.
- Exaggerating their achievements and undermining other people's achievements, like taking credit for someone else's work.
- Pretending to be something they are not, especially when it comes to things that make them look better, like being wealthy or highly skilled.
- Fabricating lies about their personal life and background, like where they grew up or went on holiday.

The Difference Between Narcissistic and Normal Lies

The primary difference between a "normal" lie and a narcissistic lie is that narcissists use lying as a way to boost their ego. Narcissists will do what they have to in order to keep up their appearance of being superior to others, even if that means harming someone else. Normal liars are dishonest for more innocent reasons and typically have no intention of harming anyone with their lies. In contrast, narcissistic liars always have an ulterior motive behind their lies, which is usually to make themselves look good at the expense of everyone else.

How To Confront A Narcissistic Liar?

If you suspect someone in your life may be a narcissistic liar, you can always confront them about it. However, bear in mind that this might not always work because narcissists are masters at minimizing their mistakes and manipulating others to go along with what they say. Here are a few ways to confront a narcissistic liar.

- **Use their own tactics against them**

The best way to address a narcissistic liar is to give them a taste of their own medicine. Narcissists always want to remain in control, which is why they actively seek out people who are agreeable, easy to manipulate, and won't cause problems. Instead of letting yourself be bullied into submission, stand up for yourself by using the same tactics that they are using on you. Make them uncomfortable by calling their honesty to question, questioning their intelligence, or shouting back. Using their own tactics against them will make them lash out, so keep this in mind when you stand up to them.

- **Gather evidence**

Remember that narcissists are skilled at brushing off their mistakes and convincing others that they're telling the truth. This means it's not going to be effective if you just call them out on their dishonesty. You need to gather evidence that proves they are lying and present your case in a clear and concise manner.

- **Indirect communication**

A safer way to confront a narcissist is with indirect communication. Try and send them a text or an email instead of confronting them in person to avoid them interrupting or talking over you. If they won't admit that they were wrong, it's best to keep your distance from them if possible – their lies are only going to negatively impact you in the long run.

- **Avoid accusations**

While it's important to confront the narcissist, it's also important not to be accusatory. This will only make it more difficult for them to recognize that they're in the wrong. Make sure you stay calm and don't let the narcissistic liar get under your skin.

Why Confronting A Narcissistic Liar Can Be Difficult

It is difficult to confront narcissistic liars because they lie without remorse and because their NPD makes it difficult for them to change their behavior. Confronting them might only lead to an ugly outburst because they might not be able to acknowledge that what they've said or done has hurt someone else. If you confront them about inconsistencies in their stories, they will likely shift the blame to you or someone else and deny any responsibility for their actions. They might also use projection to accuse you of the dishonesty they're guilty of. For example, deflecting and accusing you of lying or trying to hurt them instead of owning their wrongdoing.

IN SUMMARY

Understanding the psychology behind lying will make it easier to deal with a liar in your life. People lie for many reasons, and they range anywhere from the need to spare the feelings of someone they love to sociopathic tendencies. The true power in dealing with lies comes from when you learn how to recognize them for what they are and separate yourself from the behavior in a way that protects your mental, emotional, and physical well-being.

The next chapter will address managing body language and understanding mirroring tactics.

CHAPTER 7

MANAGING BODY LANGUAGE AND UNDERSTANDING MIRRORING

Body language is a very powerful tool. We had body language before we had speech, and apparently, 80% of what you understand in a conversation is read through the body, not the words.
Deborah Bull

Understanding body language gives you the ability to decipher what other people are truly saying and feeling, especially those looking to manipulate you, like narcissists. Body language also lets you understand your feelings and reactions toward others. You can use body language to improve your overall confidence in yourself and communication with the world.

BODY LANGUAGE BASICS

While communication is the key to success in both professional and personal relationships, your nonverbal cues speak even louder. Body language is essential for understanding others and yourself. Nonverbal cues provide us with information about how other people are feeling in any given situation. Body language is a crucial way to express emotions or intentions. While understanding body language is valuable, paying attention to the context of the nonverbal cues is also important.

WHAT IS BODY LANGUAGE?

Body language is the nonverbal component of communication used to show our true feelings and make our messages more impactful. Communication consists of so much more than just words, and unspoken cues like tone of voice, posture, facial expressions, and gestures all play an important part – even things that are barely noticeable, like a brief nod of the head or shrug of the shoulder, speak volumes. A simple example of positive body language is maintaining eye contact, which shows you're engaged and actively listening to what a person has to say. Another instance of body language with a more negative connotation is sitting or standing with your arms crossed across your chest, expressing insecurity, annoyance, or being closed off (Mind Tools Content Team, 2020).

When you read nonverbal cues, you are able to understand the complete message that someone is conveying. Understanding the basics of body language will allow you to be more aware of a person's reactions to what you say and do. You will also be able to use your own body language to appear more confident, engaging, and approachable.

The Science of Body Language

According to Mehrabian's Communication Model, only 7 percent of a message is conveyed through words, and the other 93 percent comes from body language. This is why it's so difficult to gauge sentiment when we can't see the person, like when reading an email or a text message. It is part of the reason that there is a rise in the use of emojis, even in a formal environment like business communication.

Why is understanding body language important?

Understanding body language will improve your communication in many scenarios. Here are some examples of how being aware of body language can benefit you:

- Body language makes a better first impression, and someone's first impression of you can stick with them forever. Using positive body language will help show people that you're trustworthy, genuine, and attentive.
- Body language improves your public speaking abilities because it can be used to hide feelings of nervousness, hold the audience's attention, and project confidence.
- Body language will help you excel at job interviews. Body language will help you build a better rapport with the interviewer because it will make you appear relaxed, confident, and charismatic.
- Body language helps you handle performance reviews with composure. If you're critiquing or praising a coworker's performance, your body language needs to back up your words, so the coworker doesn't feel confused about your message's intent. The same goes for when you're on the receiving end of a performance review.
- Body language allows you to navigate more effortlessly through everyday life. Awareness of your nonverbal cues will help you develop a higher emotional intelligence, positively impacting your mental health.

HOW TO READ BODY LANGUAGE

Body language speaks most of the time, whether you intend to reveal it or not. However, when assessing someone else's nonverbal cues, you must be mindful of their environment and whether there are any potential cultural differences. You might interpret the body language one way, but the gesture might mean something completely different to another person. Here are negative and positive body language examples to look out for (Cherry, 2022).

. . .

Negative Body Language Examples

If someone is displaying one or more of these negative nonverbal cues, there's a chance they're disinterested, bored, unhappy, anxious, or disengaged.

- Arms crossed across the chest.
- Standing with hands on hips.
- Minimal or tense facial expression.
- Eyes downcast and maintaining little eye contact.
- Body turned away from you.
- Writing or doodling.
- Sitting with poor posture, slumped with head downcast.
- Fidgeting, fiddling with nearby objects, or picking at clothes.
- Gazing into space.
- Rapid blinking.
- Head resting in hands.
- Nail biting.
- Sitting with locked ankles.
- Tapping or drumming their fingers or feet.

Positive Body Language Examples

These positive nonverbal cues make someone appear confident, attentive, happy, engaged, and trustworthy.

- An open, upright posture, relaxed but not slouched.
- A firm handshake (but not one that causes discomfort or becomes awkward).
- Good eye contact and holding a person's gaze for a few seconds at a time.
- Genuine smiling.
- Appropriate hand gestures when talking.

- Tilted head to indicate attentive listening.
- Body language mirroring (copying another person's body language happens unconsciously when you feel a bond with a person).
- Leaning in slightly when someone is speaking.

FACIAL EXPRESSIONS

The human face has 43 muscles, which stretch, lift, and contort into many expressions and many more microexpressions. Our faces are a part of how we communicate, but our expressions might not always come across the way we think they do. We might also be just as wrong when we read the facial expressions of others. We don't always understand when faces convey emotions like anger, fear, sadness, or joy because different facial expressions have different meanings for each individual person. What one person sees as sadness, for example, another person might see as anger or fear (Cuncic, 2021).

HOW TO READ FACIAL EXPRESSIONS

The ability to read facial expressions is an essential part of unspoken communication. If you only listen to someone's words and ignore what their face is saying, you aren't going to get the whole story. Words often don't match the emotion, and facial expressions communicate what someone is actually feeling. The benefit of understanding facial expressions is that you can collect information about how someone else is feeling and react accordingly. For example, if someone appears uninterested, they might just be tired, and it could be time to end the interaction with them.

UNIVERSAL EXPRESSIONS

According to Dr. Paul Ekman, there are 7 universal facial expressions that everyone uses, even across cultural divides. These expressions are:

- Surprise
- Anger
- Disgust
- Contempt
- Fear
- Sadness
- Happiness

However, further research (Cowen et al., 2020) has confirmed that we may actually share a total of 16 complex expressions:

- Anger
- Awe
- Amusement
- Confusion
- Concentration
- Contentment
- Contempt
- Desire
- Doubt
- Disappointment
- Elation
- Interest
- Pain
- Surprise
- Sadness
- Triumph

MICRO-EXPRESSIONS

Micro-expressions don't stick around for a long time and are almost indiscernible to a casual observer. They typically last for 0.5 to 4.0 seconds and cannot be faked. But they convey the same emotions as a longer-lasting facial expression would. Micro-expressions are often linked to emotions that a person is trying to conceal, and paying attention to these micro-expressions could reveal whether someone is being dishonest or not. However, spotting and interpreting these micro-expressions can be tricky, but it's a skill that can be learned.

IDENTIFY FACIAL EXPRESSIONS BY FACIAL FEATURE

With the number of facial expressions we convey, we tend to concentrate on different areas of the face when trying to interpret what each expression means. For example, we look at the eyes to determine if someone is angry or sad and check the mouth to see if someone is happy. Here are a few ways to identify facial expressions based on facial features.

1. Eyes

The eyes are the window to the soul and are the first place people look to determine what someone else might be feeling. The eyes can be:

- Rapid blinking (showing discomfort or distress) or blinking too little (meaning that someone is trying to control their eyes).
- Dilated (showing arousal or interest).
- Staring intensely (conveying anger or attention) or looking away (meaning discomfort or distraction).

2. Eyebrows

Eyebrows show distinctive emotional signs and are possibly as important as the eyes for depicting emotion. The eyebrows can be:

- Lowered and scrunched together, signifying anger, fear, or sadness.
- Raised and arched, displaying surprise.
- Drawn up in the inner corners, showing sadness.

3. Mouth

The mouth expresses more than just a smile and is often used to hide other emotions the face is conveying. For example, a forced smile might cover up the expression in someone's eyes. Look out for expressions like:

- An open mouth, expressing fear.
- A dropped jaw, signaling surprise.
- One side of the mouth raised, indicating contempt or hate.
- Corners that are drawn down, conveying sadness.
- Raised corners, showing happiness.
- Lip biting, which could mean anxiety.
- Covering the mouth, showing that someone could be hiding something.
- Pursed lips, indicating distaste.

USING BODY LANGUAGE TO INCREASE YOUR CONFIDENCE

People might quickly dismiss or discredit you if you look insecure and uncomfortable. However, appearing more confident will likely result in people giving you the respect and attention you deserve. Confident body language is a fundamental part of how we communicate, and how you carry yourself speaks volumes to the outside world. That is why it's so important to learn how to appear more confident, even when you're not feeling that way – *fake it till you make it*. Many of us struggle with self-doubt and lack self-confidence. The good news is that you can learn how to act more confidently, and it all starts with small changes to your mindset and physical movements. Acting more confidently will eventually make you genuinely feel comfortable with yourself and at ease in social situations. Here are some ways to adjust your body language so that you radiate confidence (Team Tony, 2021):

- **Align your shoulders**

Slouching indicates a lack of sincerity and self-assurance. Standing up straight, pushing your shoulders back slightly, and opening your chest will automatically make you look more confident. Keep your shoulders even and square them with the person you're speaking to. It's important to point your body where you want your attention to go. If you're talking to someone, but your body is facing the door, it comes across as if you're not interested in the conversation or you're uncomfortable or discourteous. Squaring your shoulders to the person you're engaging with shows confidence and interest and helps you form an instant bond.

- **Stop fidgeting**

One of the biggest confident body language destroyers is fidgeting – tugging on your clothes, touching your face, playing with your jewelry, or fiddling with objects around you is a dead giveaway that you feel out of place and anxious. If you find that you fidget a lot, try and relax. Fold your hands on top of the surface in front of you or on your lap, and work on staying present in the moment.

- **Steeple your hands**

A hand steeple is one of the most confident hand gestures. The hand steeple (resembling the steeple of a building) involves placing your fingers together to form a point without your palms touching. If you steeple in the chest area, it indicates that you're confident in what you're saying. If you steeple in the lap area, it shows that you are listening attentively.

- **Make eye contact**

Eye contact is one of the most effective aspects of confident body language. It shows that you are a self-assured, caring person. A good rule to follow is the 80/20 rule; 80 percent of the time, you want to be meeting the other person's gaze, and 20 percent of the time, your eyes wander as you think about your answer. Good eye contact ensures that the other person feels like you are engaged in the conversation.

- **Shake hands firmly**

A firm handshake sets the tone for your interaction with another person. Start by holding your hand vertically with your fingers and thumb extended upright. Approach their hand as evenly as possible. When someone's hand faces up, it shows that they're submissive. When their hand faces down, it shows that they want to control you. When you shake the person's hand, make a close, assertive connection where the web of your hand meets theirs. If you want to take the confidence further, "anchor" the handshake by using your other hand to gently touch the person on the forearm. When done correctly, this communicates that you are fully committed to engaging with that person.

- **Walk with ease**

The way you walk expresses whether you're insecure, happy, nervous, relaxed, in a rush, or upset. Walk upright and slowly with your arms held loose at your sides. Keep your shoulders back and your chin slightly lifted. Pair this with an open, friendly expression, and be ready to shake hands when you encounter other people. Your confident body language will attract others to you.

- **Create confidence-building habits**

Once you've improved your body language in the moment (fake it), you can work on changing your habits to build real confidence (make it). The three most powerful habits are priming, visualization, and affirmations. Priming is a morning routine that incorporates aspects of meditation and psychology to begin your day in a confident and empowered state. Visualization is a form of mental conditioning where you create mental pictures in your mind of an outcome you want to achieve. You can take visualizations to the next level with incantations or affirmations that promote confidence.

- **Master your emotions**

Truly mastering confidence starts with the ability to control your emotions. If you let small annoyances upset you or live in a constant state of fear, your confidence will be overruled by your emotions. Start by recognizing your feelings without letting the emotion overtake you. Ask yourself what the emotion is communicating to you, and take steps toward bringing balance back to your state. Practice using confident body language to "trick" your brain into releasing negativity so you can replace it with positive emotions.

THE BODY LANGUAGE OF A NARCISSIST

When it comes to spotting a narcissist from their body language, it is important not to confuse them with a confident person. A confident, successful person is a pleasure to be around and makes you feel good about yourself. While a narcissist can be charming and entertaining, they often display disdainful, snobbish, or patronizing attitudes that make you feel small. Here are some of the common nonverbal cues of a narcissist (Narcissism and how to survive it, 2018):

1. When narcissists (especially males) shake your hand, they hold the shake for too long, pull the other person's arm toward them, or grip the other person's hand to the point of causing pain. This is all to throw the person they're greeting slightly off balance and assert their dominance.
2. They attempt to attract the attention of other people (especially those of the opposite gender) in a crowd by physically elevating themselves above others, for example, standing on a higher platform.
3. When narcissists use hand gestures, they gesticulate in such a way that their hands and palms typically face their own

bodies, as opposed to gesturing openly and "away from the body."

4. Narcissists raise their voices unnecessarily to make their presence known immediately.

5. Their facial expressions rarely match their words while they're praising or admiring someone else.

6. Narcissists look at other people with complete disdain and use their eyes to let people know they're not worthy of acknowledgement. They stare with cold, predatory eyes, examining your body language for signs of vulnerability (for example, blushing easily, fidgeting out of insecurity, seeking advice from others, or indecision when ordering from a menu).

7. They use emotionless language because they are only in touch with basic emotions like happiness, sadness, fear, envy, and jealousy. They don't use words associated with more nuanced emotions because they don't feel them and lack empathy toward others.

8. If another person is excited or emotional about something, the narcissist may react inappropriately by laughing when someone is upset or being completely dismissive toward someone sharing excitement about something.

9. "Normal" people smile when they first meet someone to show the other person that they are friendly and pleased to see them. However, narcissists greet people without showing any change in their facial expressions. Their tone of voice remains flat and emotionless and doesn't show that they are pleased to meet anyone.

10. Sometimes narcissists have an exaggerated way of talking. For example, talking with a foreign accent (even though they've never been overseas), being overly dramatic in their delivery as if they were on stage, talking very loudly to drown other conversations out, talking very softly, so people need to lean into them to hear, or talking very slowly so that it takes them forever to get their point across. Female

narcissists might talk in a "baby voice" to appear *cute* and express that they "need someone to take care of them."

11. If a narcissist perceives someone as a threat, they will sneer and jeer at this person, accusing them of being a *show-off* or *know-it-all*. They often do this behind the person's back by pulling faces and making insulting hand gestures.

12. Narcissists often touch others inappropriately, either sexually or to show dominance. This is a method of control, but they get extremely aggressive if someone inappropriately touches them.

13. They shove people out of the way while walking in a mall or on the street to assert dominance or push in front of others in queues without a care for the consequences.

14. Narcissists take up more physical space than necessary. For example, a male narcissist might spread their legs in a communal space. They will not move out of the way when someone tries to get past them. They do things like using the armrest on public transport and making no effort to share the space. Or setting the temperature how they like it despite other people feeling hot or cold.

15. Male narcissists will typically try to kiss females on the lips when it's inappropriate, and a cheek kiss would suffice. This is done to dominate the female. They will also often "undress" a woman with their eyes as an act of dominance to make the woman feel uncomfortable and give the narcissist the upper hand.

16. Some narcissists usually insist someone goes through the door first to let that person know they're in control of the situation. It may seem polite, but it's another act of dominance to express that they decide the order of things. On the other hand, some narcissists will push through the door first, despite there being older people or women around, to show that they're the most important.

WHY NARCISSISTS LOVE TO MIRROR YOU

Mirroring is the behavior where a person subconsciously imitates someone else's gestures, speech patterns, behaviors, or attitudes. Mirroring often occurs in social situations, like in the company of close family or friends, and often goes unnoticed by both parties. However, this behavior is also commonly used by narcissists and other emotional manipulators. Whether it's a friendship, work environment, or romantic relationship, the narcissist carefully examines you and acts accordingly. For example, if you're looking for adventure in a friendship, the narcissist will be the most exciting person in the world. If you're looking for clarity in a relationship, you won't find anyone more honest than them. Narcissists mimic all your wishes and reflect them back to you. This tactic makes you feel like they've got everything you've been searching for in a person.

However, beyond imitating the things you're searching for, they also mirror you. One of the ways narcissists do this is through physical appearance – they replicate your hairstyle, the way you talk, and how you dress, which is especially common in friendships with a same-sex narcissist. By mirroring your physical appearance, they slowly steal your identity. However, it's so subtle that it might even look like you're the one imitating them.

It's not only your appearance they copy; they can also mimic your values and character. For example, you're kind and generous, and the narcissist will begin acting the same way. You might look at them and think they're such an amazing person, but all those moral traits you see in them are actually yours that they've imitated. Narcissists are notorious for making everything about them. While you're busy appreciating their values, what they're really doing is holding up a mirror in your face. But you can't recognize these characteristics in yourself because it's all about the narcissist.

Another way narcissists mirror you is to imitate the things you enjoy. For example, you like doing yoga, and so do they. You love a certain movie, and it turns out that it's their favorite movie as well. At first, this might seem like you both have things in common, but in reality, the narcissist is just mirroring you.

Apart from being manipulative, there are three other reasons why narcissists mirror you (Narsistsiz, 2020):

1. **It's a survival tactic**

Most narcissists don't experience human emotion properly and, therefore, cannot reflect these feelings. People who lack empathy are unable to experience complicated emotions and cannot convey them through facial expressions and body language. The reason that you might not notice this in a narcissist is because they observe their surroundings carefully. They pay attention to scenarios that cause other people happiness or pain and start mirroring gestures and expressions. They learn what someone's eyes look like when they're angry or how the corners of the mouth drop when they're sad and mirror these accordingly. Because narcissists lack empathy, they also lack moral values. People don't want to be around someone that doesn't feel remorse or guilt for their actions. For narcissists, mirroring is a survival tactic because they know that the people around them won't like them if they're different.

2. **They lack an identity**

Everyone is unique and quirky. But when it comes to a narcissist, things are a little different. Many narcissists never develop a personality and therefore have no real identity. They wear a mask from a young age and never take it off. This mask appears to be charming on the outside, but it is only hiding emptiness on the inside. That means that narcissists attempt to fill this emptiness by imitating others. They try to make themselves look complete by stealing someone's hobbies, mimicking another person's smile, mirroring someone else's values, and so on.

3. **Jealousy**

When a narcissist grows envious of something that another person possesses, they get extremely upset and try to mirror it. For example, you're naturally funny and crack jokes that always make people laugh. The narcissist will attempt to mirror you by laughing and joking the way you do. You might even hear them telling other people the very same jokes you had just told. In another instance, you're a very charitable person, and other people praise you for it. Even though the narcissist feels no compassion or need to help others, they're envious of the admiration you receive for being a generous person. In their attempt to earn praise, they will mirror your kind-heartedness.

However, it's important not to be flattered by their mirroring. They are not mirroring you because they admire you; they are mirroring you for selfish reasons. True admiration is appreciating someone you think is better than you; it motivates you to try harder to improve yourself and your life. Admiration is being inspired by other people's success. On the other hand, a narcissist doesn't actually want anyone to be smarter or more talented than them, and their biggest goal is to sabotage someone's success.

IN SUMMARY

Body language is a range of nonverbal cues like posture, facial expressions, and hand gestures. Understanding body language can help you understand and interpret other people's unspoken issues or feelings. It can also help you increase your confidence, making you less of a target for narcissists and those looking to manipulate you.

In the final chapter of this book, we will cover narcissistic mind control and how to defend yourself against it.

CHAPTER 8

FLIP IT AROUND: HOW NARCISSISTS USE MIND CONTROL TO MANIPULATE YOU AND HOW YOU CAN DEFEND YOURSELF

If you don't control your mind, someone else will.
John Allston

The simple definition of mind control is persuasion and brainwashing that is done to take over a person's mind. The idea of brainwashing went viral in the 1950s when the CIA decided to wage psychological warfare against Communism. Project MKUltra (Magazine, 2017) experimented with mind control techniques by dosing people with LSD without their consent. But, it wasn't just the CIA that used "brainwashing." After 918 people died in the 1978 Jonestown Massacre, the public believed cult leaders like Jim Jones could criminally override someone's mind.

However, psychologists no longer use the term brainwashing. They talk about manipulation, coercion, influence, and persuasion. While brainwashing has been debunked, largely due to it being untestable, that's not to say that regular people aren't still in danger of being manipulated by dark psychological forces.

Mind control involves manipulative tactics that affect the brain and behavior. A large part of mind control is coercive persuasion, which is the use of different techniques to manipulate someone to do something they wouldn't normally do. Narcissists are skilled at using this technique to control you.

HOW DOES NARCISSISTIC MIND CONTROL WORK? (LANCER, 2020)

A recent study (Walton, 2019) has shed light on how the mind can be influenced by other people. This research revealed that our brains are directly affected by those around us. The primary factor is dominance. In the study using mice, the brain of the subordinate mouse synchronized with the dominant mouse. This applies to humans as well. In general, people with stronger personalities make the decisions and focus on self-gratification more than people with more submissive personalities do. The study went on to show that the more the mice engaged with one another, the more their brain activity synchronized. This shows that the longevity and intensity of a relationship affect how much influence the people close to us have.

There are two types of brain cells involved with synchrony. The first set is focused on other people's behavior, and the second is focused on our own behavior. Where we place our attention is important.

DOMINANCE VS. BALANCE IN RELATIONSHIPS

In an ideal world, friendships and personal relationships are balanced so that both parties have an equal contribution to the decision-making process. After all, it is only fair that both parties have their needs met. Each friend or partner must be able to defend themselves and negotiate on their own behalf. A healthy, interdependent relationship consists of compromise and a little give-and-take between both parties. This balance within a relationship requires autonomy, mutual respect, healthy self-esteem, and assertive communication skills.

On the other side are contrasted relationships where there is a power imbalance, like in an abusive relationship. One of the parties leads, and the other one follows. One person dominates, and the other accommodates. These relationships are defined by constant conflict and power struggles. The *dominator* is aggressive and motivated to keep control and power, while the *accommodator* is passive and motivated to keep the love and connection. Most people contain both aspects in their personality, but other people have predominantly more of one. For example, narcissists are naturally dominators, and codependents are accommodators.

HOW YOUR PARTNER CONTROLS YOUR BRAIN

Brain synchronization allows the dominant animal to lead and subordinate other animals to understand and follow its cues. This translates to relationships where the dominant partner's brain entrains the subordinate partner, whose brain synchronizes with it. The pattern only strengthens the longer the two parties interact. In some cases, one partner might be assertive and appear to have strong independence before or outside of the relationship. But once they're attached to the dominator, they increasingly put the dominant partner first and accommodate all of the dominator's needs while neglecting their own.

There are many variables at work when it comes to dominating relationships. However, brain synchronization is the aspect that makes it more difficult for the submissive person in the relationship to think and act independently and challenge the imbalance of power. The accommodator focuses on other people more than themselves. They know that they lose themselves in relationships but still adapt to other people's feelings, needs, and wants. The "other neurons" in their brains light up more frequently than their "self neurons." In contrast, the brains of dominators and narcissists light up the "self neurons" more than "other neurons."

THE MIND CONTROL TECHNIQUES NARCISSISTS USE ON YOU

According to Margaret Singer, a clinical psychologist, there are six conditions that a person must be subjected to for mind control to take place (Stines, 2019). These are:

- **Being kept in the dark**

Victims of mind control are kept in the dark and become completely unaware that they're being changed. They are psychologically manipulated to change the way they behave in order to meet the agenda of the narcissist. The end goal is for the victim to do the bidding of the manipulator by fulfilling their personal needs for power and control and even their ultimate fantasies.

- **Being controlled**

Narcissists control the victim's physical and social environment. They give the victim plenty of rules, structures, and assignments to keep them constantly on task. They may also take control over finances to ensure that the victim is dependent on them.

- **Being isolated**

Victims of mind control are made to feel powerless. The narcissist prevents the victim from engaging with their friends, family, social support, and hobbies. They put them in an environment where they feel helpless and alone. Isolating the victim makes them lose self-confidence, power, and personal autonomy. This destroys the victim's intuition. As their sense of powerlessness increases, their sense of good judgment and perception of the world decreases, resulting in a destabilized view of reality.

- **Being subjected to rewards and punishments**

The narcissist controls their victim by using rewards and punishments to promote their agenda and undermine the victim's independence and individuality. The victim is rewarded for doing what the narcissist says and punished for speaking up.

- **Being "brainwashed"**

People who use mind control create a system to promote learning their own ideology or beliefs. Good behavior, compliance, demonstrating an understanding, and accepting the beliefs are rewarded. Questioning, expressing doubt, or criticizing are met with disapproval and possible rejection. If the victim does not fall into line, they are made to feel like there is something fundamentally wrong with them doing so.

- **Being suppressed**

The system of dominating is closed, with an authoritarian structure. A narcissist won't stand for any argument from the victim and refuses any input other than their own. The narcissist never loses.

Here are a few other controlling techniques narcissists use to manipulate you.

- **Degrading the victim**

Narcissists degrade their victims and destroy their self-esteem, which makes it very difficult to resist their manipulation strategies. They do this through sarcasm, name-calling, criticizing, belittling, berating, excessive blaming, threatening, shouting, and humiliation.

- **Using the bandwagon tactic**

Narcissists use this technique to control their victims by manipulating them to go along with something because everyone is doing it. For example, a narcissist might say something like, "All your friends agree with me," to influence their victim to change their hair or how they dress.

- **Using the black-or-white technique**

Narcissists control their victims by pretending there are only two choices when there are actually a few. They get a feeling of power from this divide-and-conquer approach. A narcissist will say something like, "You're either with me or against me."

- **Using the hot-and-cold ploy**

Narcissists play hot and cold games. One week they will flatter you to get you to do whatever they want, and the next week they will use aggression. The negative moments are interspersed with positive ones, so you might not even realize that you're being controlled and manipulated.

HOW TO DEFEND YOURSELF AGAINST NARCISSISTIC MIND CONTROL AND REGAIN YOUR FREEDOM

A relationship with a narcissist is taxing on all areas of your health. However, there are several strategies you can use to defend yourself against narcissistic mind control and regain your freedom (Wood, 2022).

1. **Recognize and acknowledge the abuse**: Narcissistic relationships often have a pretense of normality. Narcissists carefully choose who they show their true colors to. They skillfully manipulate others and remain unrecognized for a long time. Too often, the victims don't realize they're in a cycle of abuse for a few years. Recognizing a narcissist's behavior as abuse is the first step toward defending yourself.
2. **Don't stoop to their level**: Narcissists are fueled by drama. They will gaslight you, deny blatant lies, and play the victim.

Don't let them pull you into this pattern. Always try and stick to the facts by keeping records of conversations. This will help prevent their manipulation.

3. **Expect a reaction**: Narcissists have inflated egos and expect the world to revolve around them. Therefore, it's important to anticipate strong reactions when you shift your focus from them to something else. Narcissists don't do well with boundaries, so when you set your boundaries and enforce them, expect the narcissist to push back or react negatively. They will attempt to manipulate you and make you feel guilty by convincing you that you are being unfair or unreasonable. Stick to your guns. If it makes it easier, write down your boundaries so you can review them often and not cave into a narcissist's demands.

4. **Don't react to their abusive tactics**: Your reaction is exactly what a narcissist wants. So, don't accept their abusive ploys as your truth. They will do everything they can to demean and discredit you. Practice your positive affirmations to undo blame and build healthy self-confidence. Stay connected with positive people that validate you for who you are.

5. **Be aware of isolation**: If you notice that you are seeing less and less of your family and friends and not participating in the things you used to enjoy, ask yourself why. Narcissists will try and isolate you because it makes it easier to control you. If you're feeling alone, don't be afraid to reach out to someone who cares, even if it's a support group.

6. **Notice if you're being love-bombed:** If you find yourself experiencing more loved than you ever have, think about why. Narcissistic manipulators use love bombing as a way to control you. They will shower you with attention and affection to make you feel important and connected.

7. **Remain mindful of your emotions and needs**: There is no equality in narcissistic relationships because everything is

always about them. It is important to be aware of this and stop it from impacting your well-being. Practice regular self-care and engage in positive social interactions. Taking care of yourself is one of the best ways to defend yourself against a narcissist.

IN SUMMARY

Narcissists are the masters of subtle control, so you don't even realize you're being manipulated. The best way to protect yourself from a narcissist's mind-control tactics is to stay informed and self-aware. Recognizing the red flags of a narcissist and the different protective techniques you can use to empower yourself is a crucial step in defending yourself against a narcissist.

In certain cases, the victims need outside intervention and help to escape the clutch of the narcissist. It is important to seek the help of a trusted friend, family member, or therapist. ***Support is essential.***

We have reached the end of *A Practical Application of Dark Psychology*. I encourage you to read the conclusion to refresh your mind with the valuable information we've covered in the last 8 chapters so that you are able to identify dark psychology tactics and defend yourself accordingly.

A MESSAGE TO YOU, THE READER!

Once upon a time, there was an author who had just published their first book. They were eager to share their work with the world and hoped to reach as many readers as possible. However, they soon realized that getting noticed on Amazon was easier said than done. The competition was fierce, and their book was getting lost in the sea of millions of other titles.

Then, a miracle happened. A reader left a glowing review of their book on Amazon, and suddenly, their book was getting more attention. More reviews started pouring in, and the author's book was being recommended to others. The author was grateful to all the readers who took the time to leave a review, as it had a significant impact on their success as an author.

Dear Reader, if you have enjoyed our book thus far, please consider leaving a review on Amazon. Your feedback is extremely important to us and can have a significant impact on our success as authors. Thank you for your support!

AFTERWORD

You have the power to heal yourself, and you need to know that. We think so often that we are helpless, but we're not. We always have the power of our minds. Claim and consciously use your power.
Louise Hay

Thank you for trusting me enough to make it through this book. I am so grateful that I was able to share my knowledge and experience with you. Dark psychology is not something that should be taken lightly. It is a real and scary reality for many people, and the trauma that follows an abusive relationship is long-lasting. You might feel like you're stuck in a toxic situation with no way out, but the methods in this book are there to guide you through this journey. It won't always be easy, but it will be worth it once you've regained your power and freedom.

Educating yourself on dark psychology and the tactics used to manipulate people is the first step toward defending yourself. Being able to identify what's happening around you will enable you to protect yourself against narcissists, gaslighters, and other malicious manipulators. It is also essential to surround yourself with people that truly have your best interests at heart. Build a strong support network and rely on these people when you need help. Additionally, keep this book close for when you feel alone, overwhelmed, and need a guiding light. This book is something to lean on, a beacon of hope for when you feel like your mind is getting too foggy.

Here is a quick recap of the main topics we covered throughout this book to remind you how much you have learned since we started this journey together.

Dark psychology encompasses the darker aspects of human nature and involves manipulation tactics to control people. It is understanding and exploiting the weaknesses of human psychology for malicious purposes. Manipulation tactics can be used by anyone but are often employed by people in positions of power to control people beneath them. Although these tactics are often considered immoral, everyone can benefit from learning about dark psychology. Understanding how dark psychology works allows you to defend yourself against its effects.

Persuasion is often confused with manipulation. However, persuasion is the process where a person's attitudes or behaviors are, without duress, influenced by communications from other people. Some common forms of persuasion are media advertisements, videos, speeches, articles, salespeople, team managers, group leaders, teachers, and counselors. There are six established principles of persuasion, which include reciprocity, scarcity, authority, consistency, liking, and social proof. Mastering these six principles will allow you to maximize your persuasion abilities. Other ways to improve your ability to persuade is to develop your communication skills, build emotional intelligence, listen attentively, use logic and reasoning to support your arguments, improve your interpersonal skills, and master the art of negotiation.

Narcissists are people that use dark psychology tactics to their advantage. Everyone falls somewhere on the narcissism scale, but it's the people on the extreme side that you need to watch out for. Narcissism is a pathological self-absorption, and people that are excessively high in narcissism have narcissistic personality disorder (NPD). A person with NPD has an enormously inflated sense of dominance that masks a fragile sense of self-esteem to the point where it interferes with their normal day-to-day life. There are five main categories of narcissism: overt, covert, antagonistic, communal, and malignant.

Narcissism is one of the three personality traits in the dark triad. The other two include machiavellianism and clinical psychopathy. People with the dark triad personality traits tend to be involved with violence and criminal activity. However, even when they don't slip into these extremes, they have the willingness to exploit people to get what they want and experience very little regret and empathy when they cause harm to others. People with dark triad traits are deceitful, manipulative, self-serving, and aggressive. Four particular behaviors indicate that someone has dark triad traits. These include the inability to sustain long-term relationships, a history of playing the victim, inconsistent and contradictory stories, and a chronic need to feel fulfilled.

When identifying a narcissist, there are some specific characteristics to look out for. A true narcissist will display 5 or more of the following characteristics: monopolizing a conversation, flaunting rules and social conventions, a fixation on appearance, being envious, having a complete disregard for others, needing an enormous amount of praise, never taking the blame, fearing abandonment, living in a fantasy world, and doing everything with strings attached. When it comes to dealing with a narcissist in your life, it is important to do the following: educate yourself, understand the abuse cycle, work on your self-esteem, speak up for yourself, set clear boundaries, practice skills that help you remain calm, find a support system, understand that narcissists need professional help, and recognize when you need help.

Gaslighting is a tool often used by narcissists. Gaslighting is a method of psychological manipulation where the abuser attempts to plant self-doubt and confusion in their victim's mind. A gaslighter's goal is to gain power and control over someone else by using methods that alter reality and force the victim to question their own judgment and innate instinct. It is often hard for people to leave these abusive narcissistic gaslighting relationships because the victim doesn't realize what they're dealing with until it's a little too late. These are typical scenarios where a narcissist uses gaslighting: citing your previous mistakes, pulling the you're-crazy card, questioning your memory, calling you over-sensitive, shifting blame to avoid accountability, accusing you of having no sense of humor, love-bombing, constantly criticizing you, pretending to have allies, feigning concern for your well-being, twisting your words, and stonewalling you.

Gaslighting is so dangerous for the victim because the gaslighter isolates you from friends and family, causes you to doubt your perceptions and reality, makes you feel insecure and vulnerable, tricks you into thinking you're going crazy, makes you worry that you're too sensitive, causes you to apologize for everything, and completely destroys your unique identity and self-esteem.

Another tool used by dark psychologists is lying. There is a big difference between occasional white lies and being a pathological liar. In general, most people show a few verbal signs that they are lying. These include filler words, cutting out contractions, frequently pausing, repeating the phrase or question, changing their pitch, and getting defensive. Some of the non-verbal hints of a liar include unusual hand gestures, fidgeting, breaking eye contact, rolling their lips, having changes in complexion, experiencing dryness or sweating, and changing the volume of their voice. A pathological liar is a chronic liar, also known as a sociopath. A pathological liar will lie for no reason at all and do so very believably. Narcissists verge on pathological liars because they say whatever they need to to keep up their appearance and lie to deliberately control their victim.

Understanding body language is essential for knowing what other people are truly saying and feeling, especially those looking to control you, like narcissists. Body language includes unspoken cues like tone of voice, posture, hand gestures, and facial expressions. Some examples of negative body language include crossed arms over the chest or fidgeting. Positive examples of body language include an open, upright posture and good eye contact. You can also use body language to enhance your self-confidence and communication skills. Some examples of body language that boost your confidence include aligning your shoulders, walking upright, making eye contact, keeping your hands still or steepled, walking with ease, shaking hands firmly, and mastering your emotions.

A common body language tactic that narcissists use is mirroring. Mirroring is when a person subconsciously imitates someone else's gestures, speech patterns, behaviors, or attitudes. Narcissists use mirroring to make themselves seem more appealing as a way to control you. It might eventually reach a point where they've completely stolen your identity. Narcissists use mirroring as a survival tactic because they lack their own identity and out of jealousy.

The concept of brain synchronization allows dominant people to control passive people. Brain synchronization makes it a lot harder for the submissive person in the relationship to stand up to the dominator and act independently. Narcissists use the following techniques to dominate you: keeping you in the dark, keeping you isolated, controlling you, subjecting you to rewards and punishments, brainwashing you, and suppressing you.

When it comes to defending yourself against a narcissist, you can use the following strategies: recognize and acknowledge the abuse, don't stoop to their level, expect a reaction, don't react to their abusive tactics, be aware of isolation, notice if you're being love-bombed, and remain mindful of your own needs.

It is often said (and I will attest to this myself) that the healing process after narcissistic abuse is typically harder than the relationship itself. This is because of the reprogramming that needs to be done, the reconditioning of the mind, body, and heart to function in an entirely different way. It's because of the overwhelming task of learning to love yourself again after being dehumanized to the point of no longer recognizing the person in the mirror. But with all the pain you need to endure, with all the lies and illusions that need to be sorted through, with all the self-reflection and honesty required when looking back on the experience, the moment you do reach the top of the mountain after the long, tough climb is worth it. When you step into the light and feel the warmth of the sun on your face for the first time in a while, when your breath is no longer heavy, and your lungs expand in size, when your heart is lighter, and you're able to truly smile again, that is the moment when everything you've been through will prove its worth. It is at this moment that you realize you've finally made it – and I promise you, that moment will come.

Please remember that you are never alone. There is always support. All you need to do is reach out to a therapist or someone who cares whenever you feel you need help.

If you enjoyed this book, please feel free to leave a review on Amazon so that other people looking for ways to use dark psychology to defend themselves can find the book and reclaim their freedom and power.

REFERENCES

10 narcissistic traits- how to tell if someone is a narcissist. Applied Behavior Analysis Programs Guide. (n.d.). Retrieved January 15, 2023, from https://www.appliedbehavioranalysisprograms.com/lists/five-signs-narcissism/

Allen, N. (2022, December 23). The dark triad: 3 dark personality types psychologists say to avoid. mindbodygreen. Retrieved January 11, 2023, from https://www.mindbodygreen.com/articles/dark-triad-personality-types#mbg-2rhqGLtleL

BetterHelp Editorial Team. (2022, September 2). How to leave a narcissist when you can't make it work any longer. BetterHelp. Retrieved January 4, 2023, from https://www.betterhelp.com/advice/how-to/how-to-leave-a-narcissist-when-you-cant-make-it-work-any-longer/

Body language. Narcissism and how to survive it. (2018, March 13). Retrieved January 15, 2023, from http://narcissistory.com/?p=437

Bonchay, B. (2016, December 29). The 8 most common NARC-sadistic conversation control tactics. Thought Catalog. Retrieved January 1, 2023, from https://thoughtcatalog.com/bree-bonchay/2016/12/the-8-most-common-narc-sadistic-conversation-control-tactics/#:~:text=Narcissists%20use%20the%20silent%20treatment,accountability%20for%20their%20wrong%2Ddoings.

Booth, S. (2022, December 13). People with 'dark triad' personality traits are manipulative and lack empathy-here's how to steer clear. Health. Retrieved January 2, 2023, from https://www.health.com/condition/antisocial-personality-disorder/dark-triad

Bradberry, T. (2016, February 16). How to be persuasive - 15 secrets of persuasive people. World Economic Forum. Retrieved December 3, 2022, from https://www.weforum.org/agenda/2020/02/how-to-be-persuasive-secrets/

Brennan, D. (2021, October 25). What is pathological lying, and can it be treated? WebMD. Retrieved January 3, 2023, from https://www.webmd.com/mental-health/what-to-know-pathological-liars

Brennan, D. (2022, December 2). Narcissism: 5 signs to help you spot narcissistic behavior. WebMD. Retrieved December 15, 2022, from https://www.webmd.com/mental-health/narcissism-symptoms-signs

Buffalmano, L. (2019). Dark psychology 101: Summary & review. Power Dynamics™. Retrieved December 15, 2022, from https://thepowermoves.com/dark-psychology-101/

Buffalmano, L. (2019). Dark psychology: 7 ways to manipulate people. Power Dynamics™. Retrieved December 15, 2022, from https://thepowermoves.com/dark-psychology/

Cherry, K. (2022, March 29). What is persuasion? Verywell Mind. Retrieved December 8,

2022, from https://www.verywellmind.com/what-is-persuasion-2795892#:~:text=Persuasion%20is%20a%20process%20in,whether%20to%20act%20on%20it

Cherry, K. (2022, September 8). How to read body language and facial expressions. Verywell Mind. Retrieved January 7, 2023, from https://www.verywellmind.com/understand-body-language-and-facial-expressions-4147228

Cowen, A. S., Keltner, D., Schroff, F., Jou, B., Adam, H., & Prasad, G. (2020, December 16). Sixteen facial expressions occur in similar contexts worldwide. Nature News. Retrieved January 12, 2023, from https://www.nature.com/articles/s41586-020-3037-7

Cuncic, A. (2021, March 30). How to better understand facial expressions. Verywell Mind. Retrieved January 8, 2023, from https://www.verywellmind.com/understanding-emotions-through-facial-expressions-3024851

DiGiulio, S. (2018, July 13). What is gaslighting? NBCNews.com. Retrieved January 5, 2023, from https://www.nbcnews.com/better/health/what-gaslighting-how-do-you-know-if-it-s-happening-ncna890866

Docan-Morgan, T. (2021, November 17). How often do people lie? UW. Retrieved January 8, 2023, from https://www.uwlax.edu/currents/how-often-do-people-lie/

Duradonib, M., Vagnolic, L., Veselka, L., Torres-Marín, J., Paulhus, D. L., Martin, R. A., Batey, M., Bereczkei, T., Besser, A., & Dionigi, A. (2022, June 10). Humor and the dark triad: Relationships among narcissism, Machiavellianism, psychopathy and comic styles. Personality and Individual Differences. Retrieved January 10, 2023, from https://www.sciencedirect.com/science/article/abs/pii/S0191886922002719

Firestone, L. (2022, January 19). Why is it so hard to leave a narcissist? Psychology Today. Retrieved December 15, 2022, from https://www.psychologytoday.com/za/blog/compassion-matters/202201/why-is-it-so-hard-leave-narcissist

Gillihan, S. J. (2018, November 14). When is it gaslighting and when is it not? Psychology Today. Retrieved December 29, 2022, from https://www.psychologytoday.com/us/blog/think-act-be/201811/when-is-it-gaslighting-and-when-is-it-not

Gordon, S. (2022, November 7). Ways to tell if someone is gaslighting you. Verywell Mind. Retrieved December 20, 2022, from https://www.verywellmind.com/is-someone-gaslighting-you-4147470

Green, A., & Charles, K. (2019, April 28). Voicing the victims of narcissistic partners: A ... - sage journals. Retrieved January 1, 2023, from https://journals.sagepub.com/doi/full/10.1177/2158244019846693

Harris, S. (2022, September 15). How to know when someone is lying to you: Lovetoknow Health & Wellness. LoveToKnow. Retrieved January 7, 2023, from https://www.lovetoknowhealth.com/well-being/verbal-signs-of-lying

How to tell if someone is gaslighting you. Newport Institute. (2021, November 4). Retrieved January 15, 2023, from https://www.newportinstitute.com/resources/mental-health/what_is_gaslighting_abuse/

Indeed Editorial Team. (2021, September 7). What is persuasion? definition, examples and how it works. Indeed. Retrieved December 15, 2022, from https://in.indeed.-com/career-advice/career-development/what-is-persuasion

Indeed Editorial Team. (2021, September 7). What is persuasion? definition, examples and how it works. Indeed. Retrieved December 15, 2022, from https://in.indeed.-com/career-advice/career-development/what-is-persuasion

Jalili, C. (2018, November 30). How to tell if someone is lying to you, according to experts. Time. Retrieved January 6, 2023, from https://time.com/5443204/signs-lying-body-language-experts/

Jauk, E., Weigle, E., Lehmann, K., Benedek, M., & Neubauer, A. C. (2017, September 1). Vulnerable Narcissism Is (Mostly) a Disorder of Neuroticism. Frontiers. Retrieved December 29, 2022, from https://www.frontiersin.org/articles/10.3389/fp-syg.2017.01600/full

Juma, A. (2015, December 8). The 6 principles of influence: How to master persuasion. Medium. Retrieved December 15, 2022, from https://alyjuma.medium.com/the-6-principles-of-influence-how-to-master-persuasion-2f8c581da38b

Kacel, E. L., Ennis, N., & Pereira, D. B. (2017). Narcissistic personality disorder in Clinical Health Psychology Practice: Case studies of comorbid psychological distress and life-limiting illness. Behavioral medicine (Washington, D.C.). Retrieved December 7, 2022, from https://www.ncbi.nlm.nih.gov/pmc/articles/PMC5819598/

Lancer, D. (2020, April 3). Neuroscience explains how a narcissist can control our brain. Psychology Today. Retrieved January 10, 2023, from https://www.psychologytoday.-com/us/blog/toxic-relationships/202004/neuroscience-explains-how-narcissist-can-control-our-brain

Lane, S. (2022, February 2). Why is gaslighting so dangerous? Serenity Lane. Retrieved January 4, 2023, from https://www.serenitylanetherapy.com/blog/why-is-gaslight-ing-so-dangerous/

Lenzenweger, M. F., Clarkin, J. F., Caligor, E., Cain, N. M., & Kernberg, O. F. (2018, September 5). Malignant narcissism in relation to clinical change in borderline personality disorder: An exploratory study. Psychopathology. Retrieved January 5, 2023, from https://www.karger.com/Article/Abstract/492228

Lie-detecting software uses Real Court Case Data. University of Michigan News. (2015, December 10). Retrieved January 9, 2023, from https://news.umich.edu/lie-detect-ing-software-uses-real-court-case-data/

Loggins, B. (2022, March 24). Dark Triad personality: What it is and how to spot it. Verywell Mind. Retrieved January 3, 2023, from https://www.verywellmind.-com/what-is-the-dark-triad-personality-5217146

Lubit, R. (2002, February). The Long-Term Organizational Impact of Destructively Narcissistic Managers. JSTOR. Retrieved December 15, 2022, from https://www.js-tor.org/stable/4165819

Magazine, S. (2017, April 13). What we know about the CIA's Midcentury Mind-Control Project. Smithsonian.com. Retrieved January 5, 2023, from https://www.smithsonianmag.com/smart-news/what-we-know-about-cias-midcentury-mind-control-project-180962836/

Miller, J., Lynam, D., Vize, C., Crowe, M., & Sleep, C. (2017, February 7). Vulnerable narcissism is (mostly) a disorder of neuroticism. Wiley Online Library. Retrieved January 15, 2023, from https://onlinelibrary.wiley.com/doi/abs/10.1111/jopy.12303

Mind Tools Content Team. (2020). Home. MindTools. Retrieved January 10, 2023, from https://www.mindtools.com/pages/article/Body_Language.htm

Mind Tools Content Team. (n.d.). Home. MindTools. Retrieved January 5, 2023, from https://www.mindtools.com/ao9kek8/mehrabians-communication-model

Mrkonjić, E. (2022, April 28). What is dark psychology? Key concepts explained. Seed Scientific. Retrieved December 1, 2022, from https://seedscientific.com/psychology/what-is-dark-psychology/

Narcissism and how to survive it. (2018, March 13). *Body Language*. http://narcissistory.com/?p=437

Narsistsiz. (2020, March 29). A manipulation tactic: Mirroring. Medium. Retrieved January 7, 2023, from https://medium.com/psychology-self-healing/a-manipulation-tactic-mirroring-7ea98b66ffcf

Neumann, C. S. (2016). Psychopathy. Psychopathy - an overview | ScienceDirect Topics. Retrieved January 4, 2023, from https://www.sciencedirect.com/topics/neuroscience/psychopathy

Newman, S. (2015, April 16). 3 reasons you can't win with a narcissist. Psych Central. Retrieved January 4, 2023, from https://psychcentral.com/blog/3-reasons-you-cant-win-with-a-narcissist#4

Patterson, R. (2021, July 2). How to remember anyone's name (even if you're bad with names). College Info Geek. Retrieved December 1, 2022, from https://collegeinfogeek.com/how-to-remember-names/

Pedersen, T. (2013, July 6). Narcissists' lack of empathy tied to less gray matter. Psych Central. Retrieved December 19, 2022, from https://psychcentral.com/news/2013/07/06/narcissists-lack-of-empathy-tied-to-less-gray-matter#2

Pedersen, T. (2021, June 29). Antisocial personality disorder. Psych Central. Retrieved January 4, 2023, from https://psychcentral.com/disorders/antisocial-personality-disorder

Pedersen, T. (2022, November 2). Narcissists and housework: Issues you may run into. Psych Central. Retrieved December 19, 2022, from https://psychcentral.com/disorders/narcissistic-personality-disorder/splitting-housework-with-a-narcissist#narcissists-and-housework

Pietrangelo, A., & Link, R. (2018, August 18). How to handle a narcissist: 9 tips. Healthline. Retrieved December 22, 2022, from https://www.healthline.com/health/how-to-deal-with-a-narcissist

Raypole, C. (2022, June 21). 8 ways to deal with gaslighting. Healthline. Retrieved January 3, 2023, from https://www.healthline.com/health/how-to-deal-with-gaslighting

Rhodewalt, F. (2023, January 5). Narcissism. Encyclopædia Britannica. Retrieved January 13, 2023, from https://www.britannica.com/science/narcissism

Sadaf, S., & Bose, J. (2022, November 17). 9 common narcissist gaslighting examples we hope you never hear. Bonobology.com. Retrieved January 7, 2023, from https://www.bonobology.com/narcissist-gaslighting-examples/

Shafir, H. (2022, March 8). Narcissist gaslighting: What it is, signs, & how cope. Choosing Therapy. Retrieved January 6, 2023, from https://www.choosingtherapy.com/narcissist-gaslighting/

Singh, R. (2021, December 18). Narcissistic liar: How to deal with them. Mantra Care. Retrieved January 8, 2023, from https://mantracare.org/therapy/narcissistic/narcissistic-liar/

Sintelly App. (2021, September 6). Dark Psychology: 4 Techniques for Manipulation and Mind Control. Sintelly. Retrieved December 3, 2022, from https://sintelly.com/articles/dark-psychology-techniques-for-manipulation-and-mind-control

Smith, K. (2022, December 19). Forgiving your abuser: What it means and how to do it. Psych Central. Retrieved January 13, 2023, from https://psychcentral.com/relationships/how-do-i-forgive-my-abuser#recap

Stines, D. S. (2019, March 14). Understanding manipulative mind control and what to do about it (part 1). Psych Central. Retrieved January 5, 2023, from https://psychcentral.com/pro/recovery-expert/2019/03/understanding-manipulative-mind-control-and-what-to-do-about-it-part-1#1

Streeter, L. A., Apple, W., Olson, C., Geller, V., & Krauss, R. M. (1977, May). Pitch changes during attempted deception. Journal of personality and social psychology. Retrieved January 6, 2023, from https://pubmed.ncbi.nlm.nih.gov/874738/

T. Editors of Encyclopaedia. (2022, September 6). Narcissus. Encyclopedia Britannica. Britannica, . Retrieved December 5, 2022, from https://www.britannica.com/topic/Narcissus-Greek-mythology

Team Tony. (2021, January 21). Top 10 tips to have more confident body language. tonyrobbins.com. Retrieved January 5, 2023, from https://www.tonyrobbins.com/mind-meaning/confidence-and-charisma/

Telloian, C. (2021, September 15). How many types of narcissism are there? Psych Central. Retrieved December 28, 2022, from https://psychcentral.com/health/types-of-narcissism

Towler, D. A. (2020, December 31). Machiavellianism: What it is, how to recognize and cope with Machiavellians: CQ Net - management skills for everyone. CQ Net - Management skills for everyone! Retrieved December 15, 2022, from https://www.ckju.net/en/dossier/machiavellianism-what-it-how-recognize-and-cope-machiavellians

Vergin, J. (2019, December 13). Unbearable: Living with a narcissist – DW – 12/13/2019. dw.com. Retrieved January 2, 2023, from https://www.dw.com/en/unbearable-living-with-a-narcissist/a-51653882

Walton, A. (2019, June 21). The brains of pairs of animals synchronize during social interaction. UCLA. Retrieved January 9, 2023, from https://newsroom.ucla.edu/re-leases/brains-animal-pairs-synchronize-social-interaction

What is priming, and how can it help you succeed in life? tonyrobbins.com. (n.d.). Retrieved January 5, 2023, from https://www.tonyrobbins.com/ask-tony/priming/

Wood, K. (2022, December 27). How to beat a narcissist at their own game. Kamini Wood. Retrieved January 7, 2023, from https://www.kaminiwood.com/how-to-beat-a-narcissist-at-their-own-game/

Zajenkowski, M., & Szymaniak, K. (2019, January 23). Narcissism between facets and domains. the relationships between two types of narcissism and aspects of the big five - current psychology. SpringerLink. Retrieved December 15, 2022, from https://link.springer.com/article/10.1007/s12144-019-0147-1

Zeigler-Hillb, V., Schröder-Abéa, M., Strelan, P., Reidy, D. E., Rauthmann, J. F., Luo, Y. L. L., Lannin, D. G., Jonason, P. K., Goldring, J., Giammarco, E. A., Fatfouta, R., Eaton, J., Brown, R. P., Besser, A., Ackerman, R. A., Back, M. D., Bakker, M., Brandsma, J. M., Campbell, W. K., ... Greenwald, A. G. (2017, August 1). I'm merciful, am I not? facets of narcissism and forgiveness revisited. Journal of Research in Personality. Retrieved December 15, 2022, from https://www.sciencedirect.com/science/article/abs/pii/S0092656617300818

www.ingramcontent.com/pod-product-compliance
Lightning Source LLC
Chambersburg PA
CBHW070719130626
46553CB00005B/2059

*   9   7   9   8   9   8   6   3   6   1   7   4   1   *